Better Homes and Gardens®

ALL-TIME FAVORITE *Fruit* recipes

© 1980 by Meredith Corporation, Des Moines, Iowa.
All Rights Reserved. Printed in the United States of America.
Large-Format Edition. First Printing, 1983.
Library of Congress Catalog Card Number: 79-53045
ISBN: 0-696-01330-4

On the cover: Favorite fruit recipes include *Honeydew Fruit Salad, Orange Lemonade*, and strawberry- and orange-topped *Italian Orange Flan* (see index for recipe page numbers).

BETTER HOMES AND GARDENS® BOOKS
Editor: Gerald M. Knox
Art Director: Ernest Shelton

Food and Nutrition Editor: Doris Eby
Senior Associate Food Editor: Sharyl Heiken
Senior Food Editors: Sandra Granseth,
    Elizabeth Woolever
Associate Food Editors: Mary Cunningham,
    Joanne Johnson, Bonnie Lasater,
    Marcia Stanley, Joy Taylor, Pat Teberg
Recipe Development Editor: Marion Viall
Test Kitchen Director: Sharon Golbert
Test Kitchen Home Economists: Jean Brekke,
    Kay Cargill, Marilyn Cornelius, Maryellyn Krantz,
    Marge Steenson

Associate Art Directors: Randall Yontz,
    Neoma Alt West
Copy and Production Editors: David Kirchner,
    Lamont Olson, David Walsh
Assistant Art Director: Harry Priekulis
Senior Graphic Designer: Faith Berven
Graphic Designers: Linda Ford,
    Sheryl Veenschoten, Tom Wegner

Editor in Chief: James A. Autry
Editorial Director: Neil Kuehnl
Group Administrative Editor: Duane Gregg
Executive Art Director: William J. Yates

All-Time Favorite Fruit Recipes
Editors: Joanne Johnson, Bonnie Lasater
Copy and Production Editor: Lamont Olson
Graphic Designer: Sheryl Veenschoten

Our seal assures you that every recipe in
All-Time Favorite Fruit Recipes is endorsed
by the Better Homes and Gardens Test Kitchen.
Each recipe is tested for family appeal,
practicality, and deliciousness.

CONTENTS

Go ahead, indulge in *Berry Chiffon Pie, Fruit Strata Salad, Fruit Platter with Orange Dressing, Cranberry-Stuffed Cornish Hens, Cranberry-Orange Relish,* and *Plum-Filled Ladder Loaf* (see index for page numbers)

FRUIT FAVORITES

Sumptuous pies and desserts, sweet, juicy salads, oven-fresh breads, and more, every one featuring fruit. They're all included in this collection of recipes guaranteed to make your mouth water. You'll discover recipes that are never out of season because you choose the fruit. Then there's a tempting array of recipe favorites accompanied by a catalog of information on selecting, storing, and serving. And you'll also find a fruit preserving primer that shows you how to "put up" your favorite fruits for family and friends to enjoy year-round.

1 CHOOSE-A-FRUIT RECIPES

Use strawberries instead of raspberries in your favorite recipe? Or pears instead of apples? Why not? We chose a handful of popular recipes, substituted several fruits for the one traditionally used, and came up with dozens of new and flavorful combinations.

Fruit Bran Muffins (page 10)
Double-Crust Fruit Pie (page 15)

Four Seasons Fruit Soup

¼ cup sugar
2 tablespoons cornstarch
1¾ cups apple cider *or* apple juice
1 12-ounce can apricot nectar
4 inches stick cinnamon
4 whole cloves
3 cups desired fresh fruits★
½ cup dry white wine *or* unsweetened white grape juice

In large saucepan combine sugar and cornstarch. Stir in apple cider or juice, apricot nectar, stick cinnamon, and cloves. Cook and stir till thickened and bubbly; reduce heat. Cover and simmer for 15 minutes, stirring occasionally. Remove from heat. Stir in desired fruits and wine or grape juice. Cover soup and chill overnight. Remove cinnamon and cloves; stir well before serving. Serve soup in chilled bowls. Makes 6 servings.

★**Fruit Options:** Choose one or any combination of the following: Peeled and sliced or cut up apples, kiwis, mangoes, melons, papayas, peaches, pears, or pineapples; sliced or cut up apricots, nectarines, or plums; peeled and sectioned oranges, tangerines, or grapefruits; berries (halve large strawberries); halved and pitted dark sweet cherries; or halved and seeded grapes.

Fruit and Cheese Mold

1 6-ounce package lemon-flavored gelatin
2 cups boiling water
1 cup dry white wine
1 tablespoon lemon juice
1 cup dairy sour cream
2 cups desired fresh fruits★
½ cup shredded cheddar, Swiss, *or* monterey jack cheese (2 ounces)
Lettuce
Fresh fruits (optional)

In large bowl dissolve gelatin in boiling water; stir in wine and lemon juice. Gradually beat gelatin mixture into sour cream. Chill till partially set (consistency of unbeaten egg whites). Fold 2 cups desired fruits and cheese into chilled mixture. Turn into 5½- or 6-cup mold. Chill gelatin mixture for several hours or overnight or till firm. Unmold onto lettuce-lined plate. If desired, garnish with additional fresh fruits. Makes 8 to 10 servings.

★**Fruit Options:** Choose one or any combination of the following: Peeled and sliced or cut up avocados, bananas, mangoes, melons (except watermelon), or peaches; sliced or cut up apples, apricots, nectarines, pears, or plums; peeled and sectioned oranges, tangerines, or grapefruits; berries (halve large strawberries); halved and pitted dark sweet cherries; or halved and seeded grapes.

Fruit Strata Salad (pictured on page 4)

2 cups shredded lettuce
6 cups desired fresh fruits★
Lemon juice
1 8-ounce carton (1 cup) flavored yogurt
½ cup shredded gruyère *or* Swiss cheese (2 ounces)
Fresh mint (optional)

Place *half* of the lettuce in bottom of large glass bowl. If necessary, brush fruits with lemon juice to prevent browning. Top with three layers of desired fruits (2 cups each). Sprinkle with remaining lettuce. Spread yogurt over top; sprinkle with shredded cheese. Cover and chill for several hours. If desired, garnish with a sprig of mint. Gently toss to serve. Makes 12 servings.

★**Fruit Options:** Choose three of the following: Peeled and sliced or cut up avocados, bananas, kiwis, mangoes, melons (except watermelon), papayas, peaches, or pineapples; sliced or cut up apples, apricots, nectarines, pears, or plums; peeled and sectioned oranges, tangerines, or grapefruits; berries (halve large strawberries); halved and pitted dark sweet cherries; or halved and seeded grapes.

Rainbow Compote

¼ **cup honey**
1 **tablespoon lemon juice**
½ **teaspoon finely shredded orange peel**
¼ **teaspoon ground cinnamon**
2 **oranges, peeled and sliced crosswise**
3 **cups desired fresh fruits★**

Combine honey, lemon juice, orange peel, and cinnamon. Drizzle over orange slices in bowl; cover and chill for several hours or overnight. Chill remaining fruits. Drain oranges; reserve liquid. Arrange oranges in bottom of glass bowl. Top with three layers of desired fruits (1 cup each). Pour reserved liquid over fruits. Makes 6 servings.

★Fruit Options: Choose three of the following: Peeled and sliced or cut up avocados, bananas, kiwis, mangoes, melons, papayas, peaches, or pineapples; sliced or cut up apples, apricots, nectarines, pears, or plums; berries (halve large strawberries); halved and pitted dark sweet cherries; or halved and seeded grapes.

Fruit Salad Toss-Up

¼ **cup sugar**
3 **tablespoons vinegar**
2 **tablespoons water**
¾ **teaspoon celery salt**
¾ **teaspoon paprika**
¾ **teaspoon dry mustard**
⅔ **cup salad oil**
6 **cups desired fresh fruits★**
6 **cups torn mixed greens**

For dressing, in saucepan combine sugar, vinegar, water, celery salt, paprika, and mustard. Heat and stir till sugar dissolves; cool. Transfer mixture to small mixer bowl. Add oil in a slow stream, beating till thick. Cover and chill. To serve, arrange desired fruits atop greens. Pour dressing over. Toss to coat. Makes 12 servings.

★Fruit Options: Choose one or any combination of the following: Peeled and sliced or cut up avocados, bananas, kiwis, mangoes, melons, papayas, peaches, or pineapples; sliced or cut up apples, apricots, nectarines, pears, or plums; peeled and sectioned oranges, tangerines, or grapefruits; berries (halve large strawberries); halved and pitted dark sweet cherries; or halved and seeded grapes.

Choose-a-Fruit Salad Platter

8 **cups desired fresh fruits★**
Lemon juice
Lettuce
Spicy Nectar Dressing and/or Strawberry-Cheese Dressing

If necessary, brush fruits with lemon juice to prevent browning. On large lettuce-lined platter arrange fruits. Serve with Spicy Nectar Dressing and/or Strawberry-Cheese Dressing. Makes 10 to 12 servings.

Spicy Nectar Dressing: In small mixer bowl combine 1 cup dairy *sour cream*, ½ cup *apricot nectar*, ½ cup *salad oil*, 2 tablespoons *sugar*, ½ teaspoon ground *cinnamon*, ½ teaspoon *paprika*, and dash *salt*. Beat till smooth. Cover and chill. Makes 2 cups.

Strawberry-Cheese Dressing: In small mixer bowl combine one 3-ounce package *cream cheese*, softened; ½ of a 10-ounce package (½ cup) frozen *strawberries*, thawed; 1 tablespoon *sugar*; 1 tablespoon *lemon juice*; and dash *salt*. Beat till smooth. Add ½ cup *salad oil* in a slow stream, beating till thick. Cover and chill. Makes 1½ cups.

★Fruit Options: Choose any combination of the following: Peeled and sliced or cut up avocados, bananas, kiwis, mangoes, melons, papayas, peaches, or pineapples; sliced or cut up apples, apricots, nectarines, pears, or plums; peeled and sectioned oranges, tangerines, or grapefruits; berries (halve large strawberries); halved and pitted dark sweet cherries; or halved and seeded grapes.

Rainbow Compote lets you choose your own fruit combinations. Our
version features layers of oranges, blueberries, honeydew melon, and strawberries.

Chef's Choice Salad

⅓ cup honey
1 teaspoon paprika
1 teaspoon dry mustard
¼ teaspoon salt
¼ cup white wine vinegar
½ cup salad oil
2 teaspoons sesame seed, toasted
3 cups desired fresh fruits★
6 cups torn mixed greens
2 cups cooked chicken, turkey, beef, *or* ham cut into strips (12 ounces)
1 cup cubed American, Swiss, brick, *or* mozzarella cheese

In small mixer bowl combine honey, paprika, mustard, and salt. Stir in vinegar. Add oil in a slow stream, beating till thick. Beat in sesame seed. Fold in desired fruits. Cover and chill for several hours. To serve, arrange greens, cooked poultry or meat, and cheese in individual salad bowls. Spoon fruit mixture over. Makes 8 servings.

★**Fruit Options:** Choose one or any combination of the following: Peeled and sliced or cut up avocados, bananas, kiwis, mangoes, melons, papayas, peaches, or pineapples; sliced or cut up apples, apricots, nectarines, pears, or plums; peeled and sectioned oranges, tangerines, or grapefruits; berries (halve large strawberries); halved and pitted dark sweet cherries; or halved and seeded grapes.

Fruit Bran Muffins (pictured on page 6)

1½ cups whole bran cereal
1 cup milk
1 beaten egg
¼ cup cooking oil
1 cup all-purpose flour
¼ to ⅓ cup sugar
2 teaspoons baking powder
½ teaspoon baking soda
½ teaspoon ground cinnamon
½ teaspoon finely shredded lemon peel
1 cup desired fresh fruits★

In medium bowl combine bran and milk; let stand 3 minutes or till liquid is absorbed. Stir in egg and oil. In another medium bowl stir together flour, sugar, baking powder, soda, cinnamon, lemon peel, and ½ teaspoon *salt*. Add bran mixture all at once to flour mixture, stirring just till moistened; batter will be thick. Fold in fruits. Fill greased or paper bake cup-lined muffin cups ⅔ full. Bake in 400° oven for 20 to 25 minutes. Makes 15 muffins.

★**Fruit Options:** Choose one or any combination of the following: Peeled and chopped apples, bananas, peaches, or pears; chopped apricots, nectarines, or plums; halved and pitted dark sweet cherries; blueberries; or raspberries.

Freewheeling Coffee Cake

4 cups desired fresh fruits★
1 cup water
2 tablespoons lemon juice
1¼ cups sugar
⅓ cup cornstarch
3 cups all-purpose flour
1 cup sugar
1 tablespoon baking powder
1 teaspoon salt
1 teaspoon ground cinnamon
¼ teaspoon ground mace
1 cup butter *or* margarine
2 slightly beaten eggs
1 cup milk
1 teaspoon vanilla
½ cup sugar
½ cup all-purpose flour
¼ cup butter *or* margarine
½ cup chopped walnuts

Combine fruits and water. Simmer, covered, about 5 minutes or till tender. Add lemon juice. Combine 1¼ cups sugar and cornstarch; stir into fruit mixture. Cook and stir till thickened and bubbly. Cool. Stir together 3 cups flour, 1 cup sugar, baking powder, salt, cinnamon, and mace. Cut in 1 cup butter or margarine till mixture resembles fine crumbs. Combine eggs, milk, and vanilla. Add all at once to flour mixture; mix till blended. Divide batter in half. Spread *half* of the batter in 13x9x2-inch baking pan. Spread cooled fruit mixture over batter. Spoon remaining batter in small mounds over filling, spreading out as much as possible. Combine ½ cup sugar and ½ cup flour. Cut in ¼ cup butter or margarine till mixture resembles coarse crumbs; stir in walnuts. Sprinkle over batter. Bake in 350° oven for 45 to 50 minutes or till cake tests done. Cool. Cut into squares.

★**Fruit Options:** Choose one or any combination of the following: Peeled and chopped apples, bananas, peaches, pears, or pineapples; chopped apricots, nectarines, or plums; peeled and cut up oranges, tangerines, or grapefruits; berries (slice strawberries; sieve blackberries and raspberries); or halved and pitted dark sweet cherries.

Baked Fish with Fruit Stuffing

1   2½- to 3-pound fresh *or* frozen
    pan-dressed fish
¼   cup chopped onion
2   tablespoons butter *or*
    margarine
2   slices bread, toasted and cut
    into ½-inch cubes (1½ cups)
1½ cups desired fresh fruits★
2   tablespoons snipped parsley
½   teaspoon dried basil, crushed
    Cooking oil
1   tablespoon cornstarch
1   tablespoon sugar
1   teaspoon instant chicken
    bouillon granules
⅓   cup dry white wine

Thaw fish, if frozen. Sprinkle cavity generously with salt and pepper. Place fish in well-greased shallow baking pan. Cook onion in butter till tender. Stir in bread cubes, ½ *cup* fruits; parsley, basil, ½ teaspoon *salt*, and dash *pepper*; mix well. Stuff fish loosely with fruit mixture; brush with oil. Cover and bake in 350° oven for 45 to 60 minutes. Meanwhile, combine cornstarch, sugar, and bouillon. Stir in wine and ⅔ cup cold *water*. Cook and stir till thickened and bubbly. Stir in remaining 1 cup fruits. Cover and simmer about 5 minutes. Serve with fish. Serves 4 to 6.

★**Fruit Options:** Choose one or any combination of the following: Peeled and sliced or cut up kiwis, mangoes, papayas, peaches, pears, or pineapples; sliced or cut up apricots or nectarines; peeled and cut up oranges, tangerines, or grapefruits; halved and pitted dark sweet cherries; or halved and seeded grapes.

Fruited Spareribs

4   pounds meaty pork spareribs,
    cut into 2-rib sections
½   cup chopped onion
½   teaspoon ground cinnamon
¼   teaspoon ground nutmeg
2   tablespoons butter *or*
    margarine
3   tablespoons brown sugar
2   tablespoons cornstarch
2   cups apple cider *or* apple juice
¼   cup vinegar
3   cups desired fresh fruits★

Sprinkle ribs with 1 teaspoon *salt* and ⅛ teaspoon *pepper*. Place, meaty side down, in shallow baking pan. Bake, uncovered, in 450° oven for 30 minutes. Drain. Turn ribs meaty side up. Lower oven temperature to 350°; continue baking 1 hour longer. Drain. For sauce, cook onion, cinnamon, and nutmeg in butter till tender. Stir in brown sugar, cornstarch, and ½ teaspoon *salt*. Stir in apple cider and vinegar. Cook and stir till bubbly. Spoon fruits and sauce over ribs. Bake 20 to 30 minutes. Serves 6.

★**Fruit Options:** Choose one or any combination of the following: Peeled and sliced or cut up apples, kiwis, mangoes, papayas, peaches, pears, or pineapples; sliced or cut up apricots, nectarines, or plums; peeled and sectioned oranges, tangerines, or grapefruits; or halved and pitted dark sweet cherries.

Harvest Meatballs

1   beaten egg
¼   cup milk
¾   cup soft bread crumbs
¼   cup chopped onion
½   teaspoon ground cinnamon
½   pound ground beef
½   pound bulk pork sausage
1½ cups chicken broth
¾   cup long grain rice
2   tablespoons snipped parsley
¼   cup butter *or* margarine
¼   cup packed brown sugar
1½ to 2 cups desired fresh fruits★
1   tablespoon cornstarch
¼   cup lemon juice
¼   cup sliced almonds

Combine egg and milk. Stir in crumbs, onion, ¼ *teaspoon* of the cinnamon, ½ teaspoon *salt*, and dash *pepper*. Add meats; mix well. Shape into 20 meatballs. Place in shallow baking pan. Bake, uncovered, in 350° oven for 30 minutes. Drain. Meanwhile, combine broth, rice, parsley, and remaining cinnamon. Bring to boiling. Cover and simmer about 15 minutes. Melt butter; stir in brown sugar. Add desired fruits; cook about 2 minutes. Combine cornstarch and ¼ cup cold *water*; stir into fruit mixture. Cook and stir till bubbly. Stir in lemon juice. Serve meatballs over rice; spoon fruit sauce over. Sprinkle with almonds. Makes 4 servings.

★**Fruit Options:** Choose one or any combination of the following: Peeled and sliced or cut up apples, kiwis, mangoes, melons (except watermelon), papayas, peaches, pears, or pineapples; sliced or cut up apricots, nectarines, or plums; or halved and seeded grapes.

Favorite Fruit Shortcake

Apricot-Banana, Blueberry, Peach, Rhubarb, *or* Strawberry Filling
2 **cups all-purpose flour**
2 **tablespoons sugar**
1 **tablespoon baking powder**
½ **teaspoon salt**
½ **cup butter *or* margarine**
1 **beaten egg**
⅔ **cup milk**
3 **tablespoons butter *or* margarine, softened (optional)**
1 **cup whipping cream**
2 **tablespoons sugar**
Toasted coconut (optional)

Prepare desired filling; set aside. Stir together flour, 2 tablespoons sugar, baking powder, and salt. Cut in ½ cup butter or margarine till mixture resembles coarse crumbs. Combine beaten egg and milk; add all at once to flour mixture. Stir just to moisten. Spread dough in greased 8x1½-inch round or an 8x8x2-inch square baking pan; build up edges slightly. Bake in 450° oven for 15 to 18 minutes (do not overbake). Cool in pan for 10 minutes. Remove from pan. Split into two layers; carefully lift off top layer. If desired, spread bottom layer with softened butter or margarine. Whip cream with 2 tablespoons sugar till stiff peaks form. Assemble cake by alternating layers of cake, filling, and whipped cream. If desired, sprinkle with toasted coconut. Serve warm. Makes 8 servings.

Apricot-Banana Filling: In medium saucepan combine 2 tablespoons *sugar* and 1 tablespoon *cornstarch*. Stir in ¾ cup unsweetened *pineapple juice*. Cook and stir till thickened and bubbly. Stir in 1 tablespoon *lemon juice* and ½ teaspoon *vanilla*. Fold in 2 cups sliced fresh *apricots* (about 8 medium) and 2 *bananas*, sliced. Set aside to cool.

Blueberry Filling: Mash 2 cups fresh *blueberries*. Stir in ¼ cup *sugar*. Fold in 2 cups fresh whole *blueberries*. Set aside.

Peach Filling: Stir together 4 cups sliced, peeled, fresh *peaches* (8 medium) and ⅓ cup *sugar*. Set aside.

Rhubarb Filling: In medium saucepan combine 3 cups fresh *rhubarb* cut into 1-inch pieces *or* one 16-ounce package frozen *rhubarb*, thawed, ½ cup *sugar*, ¼ teaspoon finely shredded *orange peel*, and ¼ cup *orange juice*. Bring to boiling. Reduce heat. Simmer about 5 minutes or just till tender. Set aside to cool.

Strawberry Filling: Stir together 6 cups fresh *strawberries*, sliced, and ¼ cup *sugar*. Set aside.

Any-Fruit Sherbet

1 **envelope unflavored gelatin**
½ **to ¾ cup sugar**
Dash salt
½ **cup water**
2 **cups desired fresh fruit puree★**
1 **13-ounce can (1⅔ cups) evaporated milk**
2 **egg whites**
¼ **cup sugar**

In large saucepan combine gelatin, ½ to ¾ cup sugar (depending on sweetness of fruit), and salt. Stir in water; heat and stir till gelatin dissolves. Stir in desired fruit puree and evaporated milk. Turn into a 9x9x2-inch pan; cover and freeze till firm. In small mixer bowl beat egg whites till soft peaks form (tips curl over); gradually add ¼ cup sugar, beating till stiff peaks form (tips stand straight). Break frozen mixture into chunks; turn into chilled large mixer bowl. Beat till fluffy. Fold in egg whites. Return to pan; cover and freeze till firm. If necessary, let stand a few minutes before serving. Makes about 1½ quarts.

★Fruit Options: Mash or blend 3 to 4 cups of one or any combination of the following to obtain 2 cups puree: Peeled and cut up apricots, avocados, bananas, kiwis, mangoes, melons, nectarines, papayas, peaches, pears, pineapples, or plums; berries (if desired, sieve to remove seeds); or pitted dark sweet cherries.

Split warm, tender layers of shortcake, then fill with whipped cream, apricots, and bananas—it adds up to our *Apricot-Banana* version of the *Favorite Fruit Shortcake*.

Old-Fashioned Fruit Cobbler

Apple, Apricot-Orange, Cherry,
Peach, Pear, *or* Rhubarb
Filling
1 **cup all-purpose flour**
2 **tablespoons sugar**
1½ **teaspoons baking powder**
¼ **teaspoon salt**
¼ **cup butter *or* margarine**
1 **slightly beaten egg**
¼ **cup milk**

Prepare desired filling; keep warm. For biscuit topper, stir together flour, sugar, baking powder, and salt. Cut in butter till mixture resembles coarse crumbs. Combine egg and milk; add all at once to flour mixture. Stir just to moisten. Turn hot filling into a 1½-quart casserole. Immediately spoon on biscuit topper in 8 mounds. Bake in 400° oven about 20 minutes. Makes 6 servings.

Apple Filling: Combine 1 cup *sugar*, 2 tablespoons all-purpose *flour*, ½ teaspoon ground *cinnamon*, and ¼ teaspoon ground *nutmeg*. Stir in 6 cups sliced, peeled *apples* (6 medium). Cook and stir over medium heat till boiling. Cover and cook about 5 minutes longer or just till tender, stirring occasionally. Stir in 1 tablespoon *lemon juice*.

Apricot-Orange Filling: Combine ½ cup *sugar*, 4 teaspoons *cornstarch*, ¼ teaspoon ground *cinnamon*, and ¼ teaspoon finely shredded *orange peel*. Stir in ½ cup unsweetened *orange juice*. Cook and stir till thickened and bubbly. Stir in 5 cups sliced fresh *apricots* (20 medium) and 1 tablespoon *butter*; heat through.

Cherry Filling: Combine 4 cups fresh *or* frozen pitted *tart red cherries*, thawed, ¾ cup *sugar*, ⅓ cup *water*, and 1 tablespoon quick-cooking *tapioca*. Let stand 15 minutes, stirring occasionally. Cook and stir till slightly thickened and bubbly. Stir in 1 tablespoon *butter*.

Peach Filling: Combine ½ cup packed *brown sugar*, 4 teaspoons *cornstarch*, and ¼ teaspoon ground *nutmeg*. Stir in ½ cup *water*. Cook and stir till thickened and bubbly. Stir in 4 cups sliced, peeled, fresh *peaches* (8 medium), 1 tablespoon *lemon juice*, and 1 tablespoon *butter*; heat through.

Pear Filling: Combine ½ cup *sugar*, 4 teaspoons *cornstarch*, ¼ teaspoon ground *cinnamon*, and ¼ teaspoon ground *mace*. Stir in ½ cup *water*. Cook and stir till bubbly. Stir in 4 cups sliced, peeled, *pears* (8 medium), 1 tablespoon *lemon juice*, and 1 tablespoon *butter*; heat through.

Rhubarb Filling: Combine 1 cup *sugar*, 2 tablespoons *cornstarch*, and ¼ teaspoon ground *cinnamon*. Stir in 4 cups fresh *rhubarb* cut into 1-inch pieces or one 20-ounce package frozen *rhubarb*, thawed, and ¼ cup *water*. Cook and stir till thickened and bubbly. Stir in 1 tablespoon *butter*.

Cinnamon Fruit Crisp

½ **cup quick-cooking rolled oats**
½ **cup packed brown sugar**
¼ **cup all-purpose flour**
½ **teaspoon ground cinnamon**
   Dash salt
¼ **cup butter *or* margarine**
5 **cups desired fresh fruits★**
2 **tablespoons granulated sugar**

In medium bowl combine oats, brown sugar, flour, cinnamon, and salt. Cut in butter or margarine till mixture resembles coarse crumbs; set aside. Place desired fruits in 10x6x2-inch baking dish. Sprinkle with granulated sugar. Sprinkle oat mixture over fruit. Bake in 350° oven for 30 to 35 minutes or till fruit is tender. If desired, serve warm with ice cream or whipped cream. Makes 6 servings.

★Fruit Options: Choose one or any combination of the following: Peeled and sliced apples, bananas, mangoes, papayas, peaches, pears, or pineapples; sliced apricots or nectarines; or peeled and sectioned oranges, tangerines, or grapefruits. (If fruit is very ripe or juicy, toss with 1 to 2 tablespoons all-purpose *flour*.)

Double-Crust Fruit Pie (pictured on page 6)

2 cups all-purpose flour
1 teaspoon salt
⅔ cup shortening *or* lard
6 to 7 tablespoons cold water
   Fruit Cup, Apple, Apricot,
      Black *or* Red Raspberry,
      Blueberry, Cherry,
      Gooseberry, Peach,
      Pineapple, *or* Rhubarb-
      Strawberry Filling
1 tablespoon butter *or* margarine
   Milk
   Sugar

Stir together flour and salt. Cut in shortening till pieces are the size of small peas. Sprinkle *1 tablespoon* water over part of the flour mixture; gently toss. Push to side of bowl. Repeat till all is moistened. Form into 2 balls. On lightly floured surface roll one ball into 12-inch circle. Line a 9-inch pie plate. Trim even with rim of pie plate. For top crust, roll out second ball of dough; cut slits. Prepare desired filling; place in pie shell. Dot with butter. Top with pastry for top crust. Trim ½ inch beyond edge of pie plate. Tuck extra pastry under bottom crust; flute. Brush with milk; sprinkle with sugar. Cover edge with foil. Bake in 375° oven for 20 minutes. Remove foil; bake for 20 to 30 minutes longer. Cool.

Fruit Cup Filling: Combine ¾ cup *sugar*, ¼ cup quick-cooking *tapioca*, ¼ teaspoon ground *cinnamon*, ¼ teaspoon ground *nutmeg*, and dash *salt*. Add 2 cups diced, peeled fresh *peaches* (4 medium), 2 cups diced, peeled fresh *pears* (4 medium), 1 cup *seedless green grapes*, and 1 tablespoon *lemon juice*; toss. Let stand 15 minutes.

Apple Filling: Combine 1 cup *sugar*, 2 tablespoons all-purpose *flour*, ½ teaspoon ground *cinnamon*, and dash ground *nutmeg*. Add 6 cups peeled and thinly sliced *cooking apples* (6 medium); toss.

Apricot Filling: Combine 1 cup *sugar*, ¼ cup all-purpose *flour*, and ⅛ teaspoon ground *nutmeg*. Sprinkle 4 cups sliced fresh *apricots* (16 medium) with 1 tablespoon *lemon juice*. Add apricots to sugar mixture; toss.

Black or Red Raspberry Filling: Combine 1 cup *sugar*, 2 tablespoons *cornstarch*, and dash *salt*. Add 4 cups fresh *or* frozen, lightly sweetened *black or red raspberries*, thawed (20 ounces); toss.

Blueberry Filling: Combine 1 cup *sugar*, ¼ cup all-purpose *flour*, ½ teaspoon finely shredded *lemon peel*, and dash *salt*. Add 5 cups fresh or frozen *blueberries* (25 ounces), thawed, and 2 teaspoons *lemon juice*; toss. (If using frozen blueberries, increase the all-purpose flour to ⅓ *cup*.)

Cherry Filling: Combine 1 cup *sugar*, 3 tablespoons quick-cooking *tapioca*, and dash *salt*. Add 4 cups fresh or frozen pitted *tart red cherries* (20 ounces), thawed, and 4 drops *almond extract*; toss. Let stand 15 minutes; stir occasionally.

Gooseberry Filling: Combine ⅔ to 1 cup *sugar*, ¼ cup all-purpose *flour*, and dash *salt*. Add 4 cups fresh *gooseberries* or two 16-ounce cans *gooseberries*, drained; toss. (If using canned gooseberries, reduce flour to *3 tablespoons*.)

Peach Filling: Combine ¾ cup *sugar*, 3 tablespoons all-purpose *flour*, ¼ teaspoon ground *nutmeg*, and dash *salt*. Add 5 cups sliced, peeled fresh *peaches* (10 medium); toss.

Pineapple Filling: Combine ¾ cup *sugar*, 3 tablespoons quick-cooking *tapioca*, and dash *salt*. Add 4 cups fresh *pineapple* cut into ¾-inch pieces and 1 tablespoon *lemon juice*; toss. Let stand 15 minutes.

Rhubarb-Strawberry Filling: Combine 1¼ to 1½ cups *sugar*, 3 tablespoons quick-cooking *tapioca*, ¼ teaspoon *salt*, and ¼ teaspoon ground *nutmeg*. Add 3 cups fresh *rhubarb* cut into ½-inch pieces *or* one 16-ounce package frozen *rhubarb*, thawed, and 2 cups fresh *or* frozen unsweetened *strawberries*, thawed and sliced; toss to mix. Let mixture stand 15 minutes.

2 COOK'S CATALOG OF FRUITS

Learn how to choose and use fruits to their best advantage. We've assembled this catalog to show cooks how to select, store, and serve all kinds of fruits, from the familiar apple to the unusual ugli fruit.

Fruit-Filled Melon Bowls (page 50)
Halibut Veronique (page 44)

Apples

Selecting: Choose apples that are firm and well-colored for their variety. Firmness is especially important, because apples that yield to slight pressure on the skin are overripe and often have a mealy or mushy texture. The skin should be smooth and relatively free of bruises, because these areas can become decay spots. Varieties shown here, clockwise from top, are: Idared, R.I. Greening, Red Delicious, Golden Delicious, Granny Smith, Empire, Rome Beauty, Spartan, and Newtown Pippin. Apples are available throughout the year.

Storing: Apples need to be kept cold because warm temperatures cause a rapid loss of crispness and flavor. Store in the refrigerator or an equally cool place if purchased in bulk. If stored at room temperature for any length of time, apples tend to become overripe and mealy.

Serving: For snacks or in salads, crisp varieties such as Red Delicious, Empire, or McIntosh are preferred. Baking apples should be firm varieties such as Rome Beauty, Granny Smith, and R.I. Greening. Beacon, Newtown Pippin, and Fenton are excellent for making applesauce. Treat cut apples with ascorbic acid color keeper or citrus juice to prevent discoloration.

Gruyère-Apple Spread

1 8-ounce package cream cheese
1 cup shredded gruyère cheese *or* monterey jack cheese (4 ounces)
1 tablespoon milk
2 teaspoons prepared mustard
⅓ cup finely shredded, peeled apple
2 tablespoons finely chopped pecans
2 teaspoons snipped chives
   Assorted crackers

In small mixer bowl combine cream cheese and gruyère or monterey jack cheese; bring to room temperature. Add milk and prepared mustard; beat with electric mixer till blended. Stir in apple, pecans, and chives. Turn into serving bowl and cover; chill for 1 hour. If desired, garnish spread with additional snipped chives. Serve with assorted crackers. Makes 2¼ cups spread.

Cider Salad Mold

4 cups apple cider *or* apple juice
4 inches stick cinnamon
4 whole cloves
1 6-ounce package lemon-
    flavored gelatin
1 medium orange, peeled and
    sectioned
1 medium apple, cored and
    diced (1 cup)
  Lettuce
  Mayonnaise *or* salad dressing

In large saucepan combine cider, cinnamon, and cloves. Simmer, covered, for 15 minutes; strain. Dissolve gelatin in hot cider. Pour *1 cup* of the cider mixture into 5½-cup ring mold. Chill till partially set (consistency of unbeaten egg whites). Keep remaining gelatin at room temperature. Arrange orange sections over first layer of gelatin in mold; chill till almost firm.

Meanwhile, chill remaining gelatin mixture till partially set; fold in apple. Carefully pour gelatin with apple over orange layer. Chill for several hours or overnight or till firm. Unmold onto lettuce-lined plate. Serve with mayonnaise or salad dressing. Makes 8 to 10 servings.

Waldorf Salad

4 medium apples
1 tablespoon lemon juice
½ cup chopped celery
½ cup seeded, halved grapes
½ cup chopped walnuts
¼ cup raisins
½ cup mayonnaise *or* salad
    dressing
1 tablespoon sugar
½ teaspoon lemon juice
½ cup whipping cream
  Ground nutmeg

Core and dice apples. In large bowl sprinkle apples with 1 tablespoon lemon juice. Add celery, grapes, walnuts, and raisins. In small bowl combine mayonnaise or salad dressing, sugar, and ½ teaspoon lemon juice. Whip cream just till soft peaks form. Fold whipped cream into the mayonnaise mixture; spoon over apple mixture. Sprinkle lightly with nutmeg. Cover and chill. To serve, fold dressing into fruit mixture. Makes 8 to 10 servings.

Applesauce

4 medium cooking apples,
    peeled, cored, and quartered
⅓ to ½ cup water
2 inches stick cinnamon
2 to 4 tablespoons sugar

In medium saucepan combine apples, water, and cinnamon. Bring to boiling. Reduce heat; cover and simmer for 8 to 10 minutes or till tender. Remove stick cinnamon. Mash apples with potato masher till smooth. Stir in desired amount of sugar. Serve warm or cold. Makes 1½ cups.

Chunk-Style Applesauce: Use ingredients as listed above. In medium saucepan combine apples, water, cinnamon, and sugar. Bring to boiling; reduce heat. Cover and simmer for 8 to 10 minutes or till tender. Remove cinnamon. If desired, mash slightly. Makes 1½ cups.

Cinnamon Apple Rings

2 cups water
½ cup red cinnamon candies
¼ cup sugar
4 small cooking apples, cored
    and cut crosswise into rings
    ½ inch thick

For syrup, in 10-inch skillet combine water, candies and sugar. Cook and stir over medium heat till candies dissolve and liquid boils. Add apple rings to syrup. Simmer, uncovered, for 15 to 20 minutes or till tender, stirring and spooning syrup over apples occasionally. Cool apple rings in syrup. Drain to serve. Makes about 3 cups.

Spiced Apple Nuggets

1½ cups all-purpose flour
½ cup sugar
2 teaspoons baking powder
½ teaspoon salt
½ teaspoon ground cinnamon
¼ teaspoon ground nutmeg
1 beaten egg
⅓ cup cooking oil
¼ cup milk
1 medium apple, peeled, cored, and finely chopped (1 cup)
⅓ cup sugar
½ teaspoon ground cinnamon
½ teaspoon ground nutmeg
¼ cup butter *or* margarine, melted

In large bowl stir together flour, ½ cup sugar, baking powder, salt, ½ teaspoon cinnamon, and ¼ teaspoon nutmeg. Make a well in center. In small bowl combine egg, oil, and milk. Add egg mixture all at once to flour mixture. Stir just till moistened; batter should be lumpy. Gently stir in apple. Fill greased or paper bake cup-lined 1¾- or 2½-inch muffin cups ⅔ full. Bake in 375° oven about 15 minutes for 1¾-inch muffins or about 20 minutes for 2½-inch muffins or till golden brown. Remove from muffin pans.

In small bowl combine ⅓ cup sugar, ½ teaspoon cinnamon, and ½ teaspoon nutmeg. Dip hot muffin tops in melted butter, then in sugar-spice mixture. Makes thirty 1¾-inch or twelve 2½-inch muffins.

Applesauce Coffee Cake

1¾ cups all-purpose flour
½ cup sugar
½ cup butter *or* margarine
2 beaten eggs
1 teaspoon vanilla
1½ teaspoons baking powder
½ teaspoon baking soda
½ teaspoon salt
1 cup chunk-style applesauce
¼ cup chopped nuts
½ teaspoon ground cinnamon

In mixing bowl stir together ¾ *cup* of the flour and the sugar; cut in butter or margarine till crumbly. Set aside ½ cup of the crumb mixture for topping. To remaining crumb mixture, add beaten eggs and vanilla; beat by hand till smooth.

Stir together remaining 1 cup flour, the baking powder, soda, and salt. Add flour mixture and applesauce alternately to creamed mixture, stirring after each addition. Turn into greased 8x8x2-inch baking pan. Stir nuts and cinnamon into reserved crumb topping; sprinkle atop coffee cake. Bake in 375° oven for 30 minutes or till done. Serve warm. Makes 1 coffee cake.

Apple Cider Stew

2 pounds beef stew meat
¼ cup all-purpose flour
2 teaspoons salt
¼ teaspoon pepper
¼ teaspoon dried thyme, crushed
3 tablespoons cooking oil
2 cups apple cider *or* apple juice
½ cup water
2 tablespoons vinegar
4 carrots, quartered and cut into thin strips
3 potatoes, peeled and quartered
2 onions, sliced
2 medium apples, cored and chopped (2 cups)
1 stalk celery, sliced

Cut meat into 1-inch cubes. In plastic bag combine flour, salt, pepper, and thyme. Add meat cubes a few at a time, shaking to coat well. In Dutch oven cook coated meat cubes ⅓ at a time, in hot oil; turn to brown evenly on all sides. Return all meat to Dutch oven. Stir in apple cider or juice, water, and vinegar. Bring to boiling; reduce heat. Cover and simmer for 1¼ to 1½ hours or till meat is nearly tender.

Add carrots, potatoes, onions, apples, and celery. Cover and continue cooking about 30 minutes longer or till vegetables and meat are tender. Makes 6 to 8 servings.

Simmer apples in a honey and spice syrup to serve with slices of
Apple and Spice Roast. The sauce complements roasted lamb, beef, and pork.

Apple and Spice Roast

1	**teaspoon ground ginger**
½	**teaspoon ground nutmeg**
½	**teaspoon ground cinnamon**
1	**4- to 5-pound leg of lamb, beef rib roast, *or* pork loin center rib roast**
¼	**cup honey**
¼	**cup water**
1	**tablespoon lemon juice**
¼	**teaspoon ground ginger**
¼	**teaspoon ground nutmeg**
¼	**teaspoon ground cinnamon**
2	**medium apples, cored and cut into wedges**
	Endive (optional)

Combine 1 teaspoon ginger, ½ teaspoon nutmeg, ½ teaspoon cinnamon, 1 teaspoon *salt*, and ⅛ teaspoon *pepper*; rub onto outside of meat. Place meat, fat side up, on rack in shallow roasting pan. Insert meat thermometer so bulb rests in thickest portion of meat and does not rest in fat or touch bone. Roast, uncovered, in 325° oven till meat reaches desired doneness. (For rare lamb or beef, roast for 2 to 2½ hours or till thermometer registers 140°. For well-done pork, roast for 2½ to 3 hours or till thermometer registers 170°.) Transfer meat to platter; let stand 15 minutes.

Meanwhile, for sauce, combine honey, water, lemon juice, and remaining spices; bring to boiling. Add apples. Cover and simmer for 8 to 10 minutes or just till tender. If desired, garnish platter with some of the apples and endive; pass remaining sauce with meat. Makes 10 to 12 servings.

Baked Apples in Wine

4 large cooking apples
¼ cup raisins
¼ cup packed brown sugar
¼ teaspoon ground nutmeg
4 teaspoons butter *or* margarine
1 cup rosé wine
½ cup dairy sour cream
  Ground nutmeg

Core apples; peel strip from top of each. Place apples in an 8x8x2-inch baking pan. Stir together raisins, brown sugar, and ¼ teaspoon nutmeg; spoon into apple centers. Top each apple with *1 teaspoon* of the butter. Pour wine into baking dish. Bake in 350° oven for 1 to 1¼ hours or till apples are tender, spooning wine over apples occasionally. Serve apples warm; top with a dollop of sour cream and a dash of additional nutmeg. Makes 4 servings.

Cheddar-Topped Poached Apples

⅓ cup sugar
3 tablespoons light molasses
2 tablespoons lemon juice
¼ teaspoon ground cinnamon
¼ teaspoon ground nutmeg
  Dash ground ginger
6 large cooking apples, peeled
    and cored
  Cheddar Whip

In 10-inch skillet combine sugar, molasses, lemon juice, spices, and 1 cup *water*; bring to boiling. Reduce heat; add apples. Cover and simmer for 10 to 15 minutes, spooning molasses mixture over apples occasionally. Turn apples over and simmer 10 to 15 minutes longer or till tender. Fill apples with Cheddar Whip. Makes 6 servings.
  Cheddar Whip: In small mixer bowl combine one 3-ounce package softened *cream cheese*, ½ cup shredded *cheddar cheese*, and 2 tablespoons *milk*. Beat till smooth.

Apple Bars

2 cups all-purpose flour
½ cup sugar
½ teaspoon baking powder
½ teaspoon salt
1 cup butter *or* margarine
2 beaten egg yolks
4 medium cooking apples,
    peeled, cored, and sliced
¾ cup sugar
¼ cup all-purpose flour
1 teaspoon ground cinnamon
1 slightly beaten egg white
  Confectioners' Icing (optional)

In medium bowl stir together 2 cups flour, ½ cup sugar, baking powder, and salt; cut in butter or margarine till crumbs are the size of small peas. Stir in egg yolks. Press *half* of the flour mixture over bottom of 15x10x1-inch baking pan. Combine apples, ¾ cup sugar, ¼ cup flour, and cinnamon; arrange over bottom crust. Crumble remaining flour mixture over apples. Brush egg white over all. Bake in 350° oven for 40 minutes. Cool. If desired, drizzle with Confectioners' Icing. Cut into bars. Makes 4 dozen bars.
  Confectioners' Icing: In small bowl combine 1 cup sifted *powdered sugar*, ¼ teaspoon *vanilla*, and enough *milk* to make of drizzling consistency (about 1½ tablespoons).

Dutch Apple Cake

4 medium cooking apples
2 eggs
1 teaspoon vanilla
1 cup cooking oil
1½ cups sugar
2 cups all-purpose flour
1 teaspoon baking soda
1 teaspoon salt
1 teaspoon ground cinnamon
1 cup finely chopped walnuts
  Confectioners' Icing (see
    recipe, above)

Peel, core, and finely chop apples. In large mixer bowl combine eggs and vanilla. Beat at high speed of electric mixer for 2 minutes or till light. Gradually add oil, beating for 2 minutes or till thick. Gradually beat in sugar. Stir together flour, baking soda, salt, and cinnamon; add flour mixture, apples, and walnuts alternately to creamed mixture, beating well after each addition. Beat at medium speed for 3 minutes.
  Turn batter into greased and floured 9-inch tube pan. Bake in 350° oven for 55 to 60 minutes or till cake tests done. Cool in pan for 10 to 15 minutes. Remove from pan; cool on wire rack. Drizzle with Confectioners' Icing.

Apple Gingerbread Cobbler

1 cup all-purpose flour
¼ cup granulated sugar
½ teaspoon baking soda
½ teaspoon baking powder
½ teaspoon ground ginger
¼ teaspoon ground nutmeg
1 slightly beaten egg
½ cup buttermilk *or* sour milk
¼ cup light molasses
2 tablespoons cooking oil
4 medium cooking apples,
    peeled, cored and sliced
½ cup packed brown sugar
1 tablespoon lemon juice
¼ teaspoon ground cinnamon
1 tablespoon cornstarch

For gingerbread, in large mixer bowl stir together flour, granulated sugar, baking soda, baking powder, ginger, nutmeg, and ¼ teaspoon *salt*. Add egg, buttermilk or sour milk, molasses, and oil; beat till smooth.

In medium saucepan combine apples, brown sugar, lemon juice, cinnamon, and ½ cup *water*. Cover and simmer for 5 minutes. Combine cornstarch and 1 tablespoon cold *water*. Stir into apple mixture. Cook and stir till thickened and bubbly. Pour hot apple mixture into 1½-quart casserole. Spoon gingerbread mixture over. Bake in 350° oven for 30 to 35 minutes or till wooden pick inserted in center of gingerbread comes out clean. If desired, serve with vanilla ice cream. Makes 8 servings.

Apple Dumplings

2¼ cups all-purpose flour
½ teaspoon salt
⅔ cup shortening
6 to 8 tablespoons cold water
6 small cooking apples, peeled
    and cored
⅔ cup sugar
¼ cup light cream
⅛ teaspoon ground nutmeg
¾ cup maple-flavored syrup
    Light cream

Stir together flour and salt. Cut in shortening till pieces are size of small peas. Sprinkle *1 tablespoon* water over part of mixture; gently toss. Push to side of bowl. Repeat till all is moistened. Form dough into a ball. On lightly floured surface, roll out into an 18x12-inch rectangle; cut into six 6-inch squares. Place an apple in center of *each* square. Combine sugar, ¼ cup cream, and nutmeg; spoon about *1½ tablespoons* mixture into center of each apple. Moisten edges of each pastry square. Fold corners of each square to center over apple; seal edges by pinching together. Place in an 11x7½x2-inch baking pan. Bake in 375° oven for 35 minutes. Pour syrup over dumplings. Bake 15 minutes longer. Serve warm with additional cream. Makes 6 dumplings.

Sour Cream Apple Pie

    Pastry for Single-Crust Pie
2 slightly beaten eggs
1 cup dairy sour cream
1 cup granulated sugar
2 tablespoons all-purpose flour
1 teaspoon vanilla
¼ teaspoon salt
3 medium cooking apples,
    peeled, cored, and coarsely
    chopped (3 cups)
3 tablespoons butter *or*
    margarine
¼ cup packed brown sugar
¼ cup all-purpose flour

Prepare and roll out pastry into a 12-inch circle. Line a 9-inch pie plate. Trim pastry to ½ inch beyond edge of pie plate. Flute edge.

In large bowl combine eggs and sour cream; stir in granulated sugar, 2 tablespoons flour, vanilla, and salt. Stir in apples. Pour apple mixture into pastry-lined pie plate. To prevent overbrowning, cover edge of pie with foil. Bake in 375° oven for 15 minutes. Meanwhile, melt butter or margarine; stir in brown sugar and ¼ cup flour. Remove foil from pie. Dot top of pie with brown sugar mixture. Bake for 20 to 25 minutes longer or till filling is set. Cool thoroughly on rack. Cover and chill.

Pastry for Single-Crust Pie: Stir together 1¼ cups all-purpose *flour* and ½ teaspoon *salt*. Cut in ⅓ cup *shortening or lard* till pieces are size of small peas. Sprinkle 1 tablespoon cold *water* over part of mixture. Gently toss. Push to side of bowl. Repeat till all is moistened, using another 2 to 3 tablespoons cold *water*. Form into ball.

Apricots

Selecting: Choose fresh apricots that are deep yellow, plump, and relatively firm. Avoid those that are unusually soft or hard, shriveled, pale, or excessively green. Characteristic flavor and sweetness develop as this fruit ripens on the tree. Because fully ripened apricots are easily damaged, they usually are shipped while slightly green. Available from May to mid-August, supplies peak during June and July.

Storing: Fully ripened apricots should be stored loosely covered in the refrigerator. Plan to use the ripe ones soon after you buy them. To ripen green apricots, store in a closed paper bag at room temperature.

Serving: Apricots are popular for out-of-hand eating and can be a tasty addition to fruit salads, main dishes, pies, and other desserts. Peeling is optional, and by no means is it essential for full enjoyment of this delicate fruit. If desired, peel by immersing in boiling water for 20 to 30 seconds. Plunge into cold water, then slip off the skins. Because fresh apricots have such a short season, the other forms in which they are marketed are important in bringing their flavor to meals throughout the year.

Apricot-Lemon Warmer

2	**12-ounce cans apricot nectar**
¼	**cup sugar**
¼	**cup lemon juice**
4	**inches stick cinnamon**
	Lemon slices (optional)
	Cinnamon sticks (optional)

In medium saucepan combine apricot nectar, sugar, lemon juice, and 4 inches stick cinnamon. Bring to boiling. Reduce heat. Cover and simmer for 20 minutes. Remove cinnamon. Pour into mugs. If desired, garnish with lemon slices and cinnamon stick stirrers. Makes about 4 (6-ounce) servings.

Orange-Apricot Freeze

2	**8-ounce cartons orange yogurt**
½	**cup sugar**
8	**fresh medium apricots, pitted and cut up** *or* **one 17-ounce can unpeeled apricot halves, drained and cut up**
⅓	**cup coarsely chopped pecans**
	Lettuce
	Pecan halves (optional)

In medium bowl stir together yogurt and sugar till blended. Fold apricots and pecans into yogurt mixture. Spoon into 8 to 10 paper bake cup-lined muffin pans. Cover and freeze till firm. To serve, peel off paper from salads. Serve on lettuce-lined plates. If desired, garnish with pecan halves. Makes 8 to 10 servings.

Apricot-Berry Marble

1 3-ounce package raspberry-flavored gelatin
2 cups fresh *or* frozen lightly sweetened red raspberries
1 3-ounce package apricot-flavored gelatin
1 cup lemon sherbet
1 tablespoon lemon juice
10 fresh medium apricots, pitted and chopped, *or* one 17-ounce can unpeeled apricot halves, drained and chopped

Dissolve raspberry gelatin in 1 cup *boiling water*. Stir in ½ cup cold *water*. Chill till partially set (consistency of unbeaten egg whites). Fold in raspberries.

Dissolve apricot gelatin in 1 cup *boiling water*. Add sherbet by spoonfuls, stirring till melted. Stir in lemon juice. Chill till partially set. Fold in chopped apricots. Alternate layers of berry and apricot gelatin mixtures in 6½-cup ring mold. Swirl with spoon to marble. Chill for several hours or overnight or till set. If desired, fill center with additional fresh or canned apricot halves and garnish with additional fresh or frozen lightly sweetened raspberries, thawed. Makes 8 to 10 servings.

Apricot Chicken au Vin

3 tablespoons sliced green onion
2 tablespoons butter *or* margarine
⅓ cup long grain rice
⅓ cup chicken broth
⅓ cup dry white wine
2 tablespoons snipped parsley
¼ teaspoon ground cinnamon
1 17-ounce can unpeeled apricot halves
¼ cup chopped toasted almonds (optional)
1 2½- to 3-pound broiler-fryer chicken
Chicken broth
2 tablespoons butter *or* margarine
4 teaspoons cornstarch
¼ cup dry white wine

Cook onion in 2 tablespoons butter till tender. Add rice, ⅓ cup chicken broth, ⅓ cup wine, parsley, cinnamon, and ¼ teaspoon *salt*. Bring to boiling; reduce heat. Cover and cook over low heat for 20 to 25 minutes. Drain apricots, reserving syrup. Chop apricots; stir into rice mixture. If desired, stir in almonds. Rinse chicken and pat dry with paper toweling. Stuff with apricot mixture. Skewer neck skin to back. Tie legs to tail; twist wing tips under back. Place chicken, breast side up, in shallow roasting pan. Roast, uncovered, in 375° oven for 1¼ to 1½ hours or till legs move easily in the sockets.

Meanwhile, add enough chicken broth (about ¼ cup) to reserved apricot syrup to measure 1 cup liquid. Melt 2 tablespoons butter. Stir in cornstarch. Stir in the 1 cup liquid and ¼ cup wine. Cook and stir till bubbly. Season to taste. Spoon some sauce over chicken during the last 10 to 15 minutes of baking time. Pass remainder. Serves 4.

Apricot Upside-Down Cake

1 8¾-ounce can unpeeled apricot halves★
⅓ cup packed brown sugar
3 tablespoons butter *or* margarine, melted
½ cup flaked coconut
Milk
⅓ cup shortening
¾ cup granulated sugar
1 egg
1½ teaspoons vanilla
1½ cups all-purpose flour
2½ teaspoons baking powder
¼ teaspoon salt

Drain apricots, reserving syrup. Combine brown sugar, butter or margarine, and *1 tablespoon* of the reserved apricot syrup; spread in a 9x9x2-inch baking pan. Sprinkle with coconut. Add enough milk (about ¼ cup) to remaining apricot syrup to measure ⅔ cup liquid. Arrange apricots, cut side up, over coconut. In small mixer bowl cream shortening and granulated sugar till light. Add egg and vanilla; beat till fluffy. Stir together flour, baking powder, and salt. Add flour mixture and the ⅔ cup liquid alternately to creamed mixture, beating well after each addition. Spread over apricot layer. Bake in 350° oven for 35 to 40 minutes. Cool in pan for 5 minutes; invert onto plate. Serve warm.

★**Note:** You can substitute 5 fresh medium *apricots*, halved and pitted, for canned apricot halves and 1 tablespoon *water* for reserved apricot syrup in topping. Use ⅔ cup *milk* in place of apricot syrup-milk mixture in batter.

Swirl layers of apricot and raspberry gelatin together in this refreshing salad.
Fill the center of *Apricot-Berry Marble* with additional apricots and raspberries.

Avocados

Selecting: *Choose avocados that appear fresh and free from bruises. Size, shape, color, and texture vary widely, but the ripeness test is the same for all varieties. Avocados yield to gentle pressure in the hand when ready to eat. Pictured clockwise from top are: Pollack, Hass, Reed, and Fuerte varieties. Pollack, a Florida variety, is large and bright green. The Hass variety, grown in California, has leathery skin that turns black when ready to eat. The Reed is a round California avocado. The Fuerte is pear-shaped with thin, green skin. The Fuerte is also from California, which produces more than 75 percent of the avocados in the United States. Avocados are available all year. Hass (the production leader), Reed, and Pollack are among summer varieties. Fuerte is the most common winter variety.*

Storing: *Keep avocados at room temperature until they reach desired softness. For faster softening, place in a closed paper or plastic bag. Refrigerate when desired softness is obtained.*

Serving: *To prepare, cut the fruit in half lengthwise, then twist gently and separate. Tap seed with sharp edge of knife; twist and lift out. Use a sharp knife to strip skin. Mash, cube, or slice avocados, but be sure to treat this versatile fruit with ascorbic acid color keeper or citrus juice to preserve its color.*

Avocado Soup

2 medium avocados, halved, seeded, peeled, and cut up
1 13¾-ounce can chicken broth
2 tablespoons dry sherry
½ teaspoon salt
¼ teaspoon onion powder
⅛ teaspoon dried dillweed
¾ cup light cream

In blender container combine avocado chunks, chicken broth, dry sherry, salt, onion powder, and dillweed. Cover and blend till smooth. Stir in light cream. Cover and chill. If desired, top each serving with avocado slices and dollops of sour cream. Makes 6 servings.

Guacamole

2 medium avocados, halved, seeded, peeled, and cut up
½ small onion, cut up
2 tablespoons lemon juice
1 clove garlic, minced
½ teaspoon salt

In blender container combine avocados, onion, lemon juice, garlic, salt, and ¼ teaspoon *pepper*; cover and blend till smooth. Serve as a dip for chips or as a sauce for main dishes. Makes about 1¼ cups.

Avocado-Citrus Salad

1 6-ounce package orange-
   pineapple-flavored gelatin
1½ cups boiling water
1 16-ounce bottle (2 cups)
   grapefruit carbonated
   beverage, chilled
2 medium avocados, halved,
   seeded, peeled, and sliced
   crosswise
1 cup grapefruit sections, cut up
   (1 large)
   Lettuce

In large bowl dissolve gelatin in boiling water. Stir in grapefruit carbonated beverage. Chill till partially set (consistency of unbeaten egg whites). Fold in avocados and grapefruit. Pour into 6½-cup ring mold. Chill for several hours or overnight or till firm. Unmold onto lettuce-lined plate. Makes 8 to 10 servings.

Avocado Salad Bowl

2 medium avocados, halved,
   seeded, and peeled
   Lemon juice
½ of a 3-ounce package cream
   cheese, softened
¼ cup mayonnaise or salad
   dressing
1 teaspoon lemon juice
⅛ teaspoon salt
⅛ teaspoon garlic powder
   Milk
6 cups torn lettuce
1 cup orange sections or one 11-
   ounce can mandarin orange
   sections, drained
1 cup alfalfa sprouts
1 small onion, sliced and
   separated into rings

Cut 1½ of the avocados into thin slices; brush with a little lemon juice and chill. For dressing, cut up remaining avocado half; place in small mixer bowl. Add cream cheese, mayonnaise or salad dressing, 1 teaspoon lemon juice, salt, and garlic powder. Beat till smooth. Stir in enough milk to obtain desired consistency (about 2 tablespoons). Cover and chill.

In salad bowl combine lettuce, orange sections, sprouts, onion, and avocado slices. Pour dressing over salad. Toss to coat. Makes 10 to 12 servings.

Marinated Shrimp in Avocado Halves

3 cups water
1 tablespoon salt
1 pound fresh or frozen shelled
   shrimp
½ cup salad oil
½ cup lemon juice or lime juice
2 tablespoons vinegar
1 tablespoon snipped chives
2 teaspoons drained capers
1 teaspoon salt
½ teaspoon dried dillweed
3 drops bottled hot pepper sauce
4 medium avocados
   Lemon juice
   Salt

Bring water and 1 tablespoon salt to boiling. Add shrimp; return to boiling. Reduce heat and simmer for 1 to 3 minutes or till shrimp turn pink. Drain.

For marinade, combine oil, ½ cup lemon or lime juice, vinegar, chives, capers, 1 teaspoon salt, dillweed, and hot pepper sauce. Add cooked shrimp; toss to coat. Cover and chill for several hours or overnight, stirring occasionally. To serve, halve unpeeled avocados; remove seeds. Brush cut surfaces with lemon juice; sprinkle with salt. Drain shrimp, reserving marinade. Spoon shrimp into avocado shells. If desired, drizzle with reserved marinade. Makes 8 appetizer or 4 main-dish servings.

Bananas

Selecting: Good quality bananas should be bright, plump, firm, and free of bruises or large blemishes. Color may range from green to yellow with brown flecks. Green bananas are underripe; those that are lightly brown-flecked are at the optimum stage of ripeness. Select bananas that are not quite ripe. They will continue ripening at home when stored at room temperature. Avoid those with grayish skin color, an indication of chill damage. Bananas are available year-round.

Storing: Store underripe bananas at room temperature. Once they have reached the desired stage of ripeness, place in the refrigerator and store for several days with no loss in quality (even though the peel will turn dark).

Serving: Bananas make good snacks and lunch box treats. Serve on cereals, in fruit salads, or desserts. To prevent browning, treat cut bananas with ascorbic acid color keeper or citrus juice. Mash overripe bananas for use in milk shakes, bread, or other baked products. For a simple dessert, bake or broil bananas that have been split lengthwise. Brush cut surfaces with a little lemon juice, dot with butter or margarine, and sprinkle with sugar and a little ground cinnamon or ground nutmeg. Bake in 350° oven for 15 to 20 minutes or broil 4 to 5 inches from heat about 5 minutes or till golden. Serve warm with cream.

Banana-Orange Drink

1½ cups milk
1 cup orange juice
1 cup orange sherbet
⅔ cup mashed ripe banana

In large mixer bowl combine milk, orange juice, orange sherbet, and mashed banana. Beat till smooth. Cover and chill. To serve, beat again and pour into 4 glasses. Makes 4 (8-ounce) servings.

Bananas Foster

4 ripe medium bananas
Lemon juice
6 tablespoons butter *or* margarine
⅔ cup packed brown sugar
Ground cinnamon
3 tablespoons crème de banana liqueur *or* light rum
3 tablespoons light rum
Vanilla ice cream

Peel bananas; bias-slice. Brush with lemon juice. In blazer pan of chafing dish melt butter over direct heat. Stir in sugar. Add bananas. Cook and stir for 3 to 4 minutes. Sprinkle with cinnamon. Drizzle 3 tablespoons liqueur or rum over all. Heat remaining rum in large ladle or small saucepan till it *almost* simmers. Ignite rum and pour over bananas. Serve immediately over ice cream. Makes 6 servings.

Peach and Banana Flambé: Prepare as above, *except* substitute 1 cup sliced, peeled *peaches* for 1 banana. Sprinkle *each* serving with 1 tablespoon toasted *coconut*.

Ladle *Peach and Banana Flambé*, a variation of *Bananas Foster*, over ice cream for a dessert that's guaranteed to dazzle. The addition of peaches gives this classic a new look.

Banana Nut Bread

⅔ cup sugar
⅓ cup shortening
2 eggs
2 tablespoons milk
1¾ cups all-purpose flour
1¼ teaspoons baking powder
¾ teaspoon salt
½ teaspoon baking soda
1 cup mashed ripe banana
¼ cup chopped pecans *or*
   walnuts

In mixer bowl cream sugar and shortening till light, scraping sides of bowl often. Add eggs, one at a time, and milk, beating till smooth and fluffy after each addition. In medium bowl stir together flour, baking powder, salt, and baking soda. Add flour mixture and mashed banana alternately to creamed mixture, beating till smooth after each addition. Gently fold in chopped nuts.

Turn batter into lightly greased 8x4x2-inch loaf pan. Bake in 350° oven 60 to 65 minutes or till wooden pick inserted near center comes out clean. Cool in pan 10 minutes. Remove from pan; cool on wire rack. Makes 1 loaf.

Frozen Chocolate Bananas

1 6-ounce package (1 cup) milk chocolate *or* semisweet chocolate pieces
2 large bananas
4 wooden sticks
½ cup chopped peanuts *or* flaked coconut

In small heavy saucepan melt chocolate over *very low heat*, stirring constantly. (Do not add any liquid.) Peel bananas; halve crosswise and insert wooden sticks. Spread chocolate over bananas, then roll in peanuts or coconut. Place on waxed paper-lined baking sheet. Freeze till firm. (If not eaten the same day, wrap in moisture-vaporproof wrap and store in freezer.) Makes 4.

Banana-Frosted Strawberry Squares

1 6-ounce package strawberry-flavored gelatin
1 10-ounce package frozen strawberries
2 medium bananas, sliced ¼ inch thick
1 4-serving-size package *instant* banana cream pudding mix
1¼ cups cold milk
½ cup dairy sour cream

Dissolve gelatin in 2 cups *boiling water*. Add frozen strawberries to gelatin; break up and stir to completely thaw strawberries. Stir in 1 cup cold *water*. Chill till partially set (consistency of unbeaten egg whites). Fold bananas into partially set gelatin. Pour into 8x8x2-inch pan. Chill till almost firm.

In mixer bowl combine pudding mix and milk; beat till smooth. Beat in sour cream. Spread pudding mixture over gelatin mixture. Chill for several hours or overnight or till firm. To serve, cut into squares. If desired, garnish with fresh strawberries. Makes 9 servings.

Banana Split Pie

Pastry for Single-Crust Pie (see recipe, page 22)
2 medium bananas
   Lemon juice
1 quart strawberry ice cream
½ of a 4½-ounce container frozen whipped dessert topping, thawed
⅓ cup maraschino cherries (12)
2 tablespoons chopped walnuts
½ cup tiny marshmallows
¼ cup semisweet chocolate pieces
2 tablespoons milk

Prepare and roll out pastry into 12-inch circle. Line a 9-inch pie plate. Trim pastry to ½ inch beyond edge. Flute; prick pastry. Bake in 450° oven for 10 to 12 minutes. Cool. Thinly slice bananas; sprinkle with lemon juice. Arrange bananas on bottom of pastry shell. Stir ice cream just to soften. Spread ice cream over bananas. Freeze till firm.

Spread dessert topping over ice cream. Top with cherries; sprinkle with walnuts. Freeze for several hours or till firm. Meanwhile, for fudge sauce, combine marshmallows, chocolate, and milk. Cook and stir over low heat till melted. Let pie stand at room temperature about 30 minutes before serving. Drizzle warm or cold fudge sauce over.

Berries

Selecting: As a general rule select berries that are plump, firm, bright, and full-colored. Avoid berries that are soft, blemished, leaky, or moldy. Pictured from top to bottom are: strawberries, boysenberries, black raspberries, blueberries, red raspberries, and gooseberries. Strawberries are the only mature berries that have stem caps attached. Size is not an indication of strawberry quality; the largest ones are not necessarily the most flavorful. The boysenberry, a variety of trailing blackberry, is similar in flavor to the raspberry but is much larger. In contrast to boysenberries and other blackberries, raspberries separate from their white core when picked. When buying blueberries, look for dark berries with a powdery bloom. Blueberry size is an indication of quality; large blueberries are deemed most desirable. The most common variety of gooseberry is amber-colored with a slight red blush. Availability of this tart berry is limited to local markets. Fresh strawberries are available all year but are in greatest supply from mid-April through mid-July. Blueberries are available from May through September with a peak in July. Other berries have shorter seasons limited to the summer months.

Storing: Store berries loosely covered in the refrigerator for no longer than a few days (except blueberries, which retain their freshness about one week). Most berries are delicate and should not be washed until you are ready to use them.

Serving: Berries are a favorite when served plain or when added to breads, salads, sauces, pies, or other desserts.

Sparkling Strawberry Punch

4 cups fresh *or* frozen unsweetened strawberries
1 32-ounce bottle cranberry juice cocktail
1 28-ounce bottle ginger ale
1 3-ounce package strawberry-flavored gelatin
1 6-ounce can frozen lemonade concentrate

Thaw strawberries, if frozen. Chill cranberry juice and ginger ale. Place berries in blender container. Cover and blend till berries are pureed. If desired, strain and discard seeds. Dissolve gelatin in 1 cup *boiling water*. Stir in lemonade concentrate. Transfer to punch bowl. Add cranberry juice cocktail, strawberry puree, and 2 cups cold *water*. Slowly pour in ginger ale. If desired, serve with ice ring with additional whole berries frozen in it. Makes 28 (4-ounce) servings.

Gooseberry Salad

1 **16-ounce can gooseberries**
1 **3-ounce package lime-flavored gelatin**
1 **3-ounce package lemon-flavored gelatin**
2 **tablespoons sugar**
1 **teaspoon vinegar**
1 **cup chopped celery**
½ **cup shredded cheddar cheese**
½ **cup chopped pecans**

Drain gooseberries, reserving syrup. Add enough water to syrup to measure 1½ cups liquid. In large saucepan combine 1½ cups liquid, gelatins, and sugar. Heat and stir till gelatin dissolves. Add vinegar and 2 cups *water*. Chill till partially set (consistency of unbeaten egg whites). Fold in gooseberries, celery, cheese, and pecans. Pour into 6½-cup mold. Chill till firm. If desired, unmold onto lettuce-lined plate. Makes 8 to 10 servings.

Blueberry-Lemon Muffins

1¾ **cups all-purpose flour**
⅔ **cup sugar**
2½ **teaspoons baking powder**
1 **teaspoon finely shredded lemon peel**
1 **beaten egg**
¾ **cup milk**
⅓ **cup cooking oil**
¾ **cup fresh *or* frozen blueberries, thawed**

In large bowl stir together flour, ⅓ *cup* of the sugar, baking powder, lemon peel, and ¾ teaspoon *salt*. Make a well in center. Combine egg, milk, and oil. Add egg mixture all at once to flour mixture. Stir just till moistened; batter should be lumpy. Drain blueberries. Carefully fold blueberries into batter. Spoon into greased or paper bake cup-lined muffin pans, filling each about ⅔ full. Bake in 400° oven for 20 to 25 minutes or till golden. Remove from pans. If desired, dip hot muffin tops in ¼ cup *melted butter*, then in remaining sugar. Makes 10 to 12 muffins.

Blueberry Buckle

1¼ **cups sugar**
½ **cup shortening**
1 **egg**
2½ **cups all-purpose flour**
2½ **teaspoons baking powder**
½ **cup milk**
2 **cups fresh *or* frozen blueberries, thawed and drained**
¼ **teaspoon ground cinnamon**
½ **cup butter *or* margarine**

In large mixer bowl cream ¾ *cup* of the sugar and the shortening till well combined. Add egg; beat well. In medium bowl stir together *2 cups* of the flour, the baking powder, and ¼ teaspoon *salt*. Add flour mixture and milk alternately to creamed mixture, beating till smooth after each addition. Spread in greased 9x9x2-inch baking pan. Top with *drained* berries. In small bowl combine remaining sugar, remaining flour, and cinnamon; cut in butter or margarine till crumbly. Sprinkle over berries. Bake in 350° oven for 45 to 50 minutes. Cut into squares. Serve warm. Makes 1 coffee cake.

Blackberry Cake

2 **cups granulated sugar**
1 **cup butter *or* margarine**
4 **eggs**
4¾ **cups all-purpose flour**
1 **teaspoon baking powder**
1 **teaspoon baking soda**
1 **cup buttermilk *or* sour milk**
1 **teaspoon vanilla**
2 **cups fresh *or* frozen unsweetened blackberries**
1½ **cups sifted powdered sugar**
Milk

In large mixer bowl cream sugar and butter or margarine till light. Add eggs, one at a time, beating after each addition. Stir together flour, baking powder, baking soda, and ½ teaspoon *salt*. Combine buttermilk and vanilla. Add buttermilk mixture and flour mixture alternately to creamed mixture, beating after each addition. Fold in berries. Spread batter in greased and floured 10-inch fluted tube pan. Bake in 350° oven for 1¼ hours. Cool in pan for 10 minutes. Invert cake onto wire rack; cool completely.

In medium bowl combine powdered sugar and enough milk to make of drizzling consistency (about 2 tablespoons). Drizzle powdered sugar mixture over cake.

Oven-fresh *Blueberry-Lemon Muffins* are full of juicy blueberries. For an extra treat, dip tops of muffins in melted butter, then in sugar.

Frosty Strawberry Squares

½ cup butter *or* margarine
1 cup all-purpose flour
½ cup chopped walnuts
¼ cup packed brown sugar
2 egg whites
2 cups sliced fresh strawberries *or* one 10-ounce package frozen strawberries, partially thawed and cut up
¾ cup granulated sugar
2 tablespoons lemon juice
1 cup whipping cream *or* one 4½-ounce carton frozen whipped dessert topping, thawed

In medium saucepan melt butter. Stir in flour, walnuts, and brown sugar. Spread evenly in 13x9x2-inch baking pan. Bake in 350° oven for 20 minutes or till lightly browned, stirring occasionally. Cool. Remove ⅓ of the crumbs; set aside. Spread remaining crumbs evenly in pan.

In large mixer bowl combine egg whites, strawberries, granulated sugar, and lemon juice. Beat at low speed of electric mixer about 2 minutes or till mixture begins to thicken. Beat at high speed for 10 to 12 minutes or till stiff peaks form. Whip cream just till soft peaks form; fold into strawberry mixture. *Or*, fold thawed dessert topping into strawberry mixture. Spread over crumbs in pan; top with remaining crumbs. Cover and freeze for 6 hours or overnight. Makes 12 servings.

Strawberries Romanoff

1 quart fresh strawberries
2 tablespoons sugar
1 pint strawberry ice cream
½ cup dairy sour cream
2 tablespoons orange liqueur

Sprinkle berries with sugar. Cover and chill. Meanwhile, stir ice cream just to soften. Fold in sour cream and liqueur. Cover and freeze for 1 hour. To serve, top each serving of berries with a dollop of ice cream mixture. Makes 6 to 8 servings.

Raspberry Frozen Yogurt

1 envelope unflavored gelatin
½ cup cold water
2 10-ounce packages frozen red raspberries, thawed
2 cups sugar
3 16-ounce cartons (6 cups) plain yogurt

In small saucepan soften unflavored gelatin in cold water. Cook and stir over low heat till gelatin dissolves. In large bowl combine gelatin mixture, *undrained* raspberries, sugar, and *1 cup* of the yogurt. Stir in remaining yogurt. Cover and chill overnight. Pour into 4-quart ice cream freezer; freeze according to manufacturer's directions. Makes 2½ quarts.

Berry Champagne Sorbet

1 cup whipping cream
½ cup sugar
1½ cups champagne
1 10-ounce package frozen strawberries *or* red raspberries, thawed
2 egg whites
¼ teaspoon cream of tartar
¼ cup sugar
Few drops red food coloring (optional)

In medium saucepan combine whipping cream and ½ cup sugar; cook and stir over medium-low heat till sugar dissolves. Cool. Stir in champagne and *undrained* strawberries or red raspberries. Pour into 8x8x2-inch pan. Cover and freeze till firm.

In small mixer bowl beat egg whites with cream of tartar till soft peaks form. Gradually add ¼ cup sugar, beating till stiff peaks form. Break up frozen mixture into chilled large mixer bowl. Beat till smooth. Fold in stiff-beaten egg whites. If desired, stir in food coloring. Return to pan. Cover and freeze till firm. Makes about 1¼ quarts.

Raspberry Dumplings

2 cups all-purpose flour
4 teaspoons baking powder
1 tablespoon sugar
¾ teaspoon salt
⅓ cup shortening
1 beaten egg
½ cup milk
1 cup fresh *or* frozen lightly
    sweetened raspberries,
    thawed
⅓ cup sugar
¼ teaspoon ground cinnamon
    Lemon Sauce

Stir together flour, baking powder, 1 tablespoon sugar, and salt; cut in shortening till mixture resembles coarse crumbs. Combine egg and milk; stir into flour mixture. Turn out onto lightly floured surface; gently knead 8 to 10 strokes. Roll out into a 15x10-inch rectangle. Cut into six 5-inch squares. Spoon berries onto squares. Combine ⅓ cup sugar and cinnamon. Sprinkle over berries. Moisten edges of each square. Fold corners of each square to center over berries; seal edges. Place on foil-lined baking sheet. Bake in 400° oven for 15 to 20 minutes. Serve warm with Lemon Sauce. Makes 6 servings.

Lemon Sauce: Combine 3 tablespoons *sugar* and 2 teaspoons *cornstarch*. Stir in ½ cup cold *water*; cook and stir till bubbly. Stir in ½ teaspoon finely shredded *lemon peel* and 1 tablespoon *lemon juice*. Cool. Fold in ½ cup frozen *whipped dessert topping*, thawed. Makes ¾ cup.

Strawberry Glacé Pie

  Pastry for Single-Crust Pie
    (see recipe, page 22)
6 cups fresh medium
    strawberries
1 cup water
¾ cup sugar
3 tablespoons cornstarch
  Few drops red food coloring
    (optional)

Prepare and roll out pastry into a 12-inch circle. Line a 9-inch pie plate. Trim pastry to ½ inch beyond edge. Flute; prick pastry. Bake in 450° oven for 10 to 12 minutes. Cool. For glaze, crush *1 cup* of the smaller berries; add water. Bring to boiling. Simmer for 2 minutes; sieve. Combine sugar and cornstarch; stir in sieved berries. Cook and stir till thickened and bubbly. If desired, stir in food coloring. Spread ¼ cup glaze over bottom and sides of pastry shell. Arrange *half* of the remaining strawberries, stem end down, in pastry shell. Spoon *half* of the remaining glaze over berries. Arrange remaining berries, stem end down, atop first layer; spoon on remaining glaze. Chill for 3 to 4 hours.

Berry Chiffon Pie (pictured on page 4)

  Pastry for Single-Crust Pie
    (see recipe, page 22)
2½ cups fresh strawberries *or*
    raspberries
¼ cup sugar
1 tablespoon lemon juice
¼ cup sugar
1 envelope unflavored gelatin
¾ cup water
2 egg whites
¼ cup sugar
½ cup whipping cream

Prepare and roll out pastry into a 12-inch circle. Line a 9-inch pie plate. Trim pastry to ½ inch beyond edge. Flute; prick pastry. Bake in 450° oven for 10 to 12 minutes. Cool. In large bowl crush enough berries to measure 1¼ cups. Stir in ¼ cup sugar and lemon juice; let stand 30 minutes. Meanwhile, combine ¼ cup sugar and gelatin. Stir in water; heat and stir till sugar and gelatin dissolve. Cool. Stir cooled gelatin mixture into berry mixture. Chill to consistency of corn syrup, stirring occasionally. Remove from refrigerator (gelatin mixture will continue to set).

Immediately begin beating egg whites till soft peaks form. Gradually add ¼ cup sugar, beating till stiff peaks form. When gelatin is partially set (consistency of unbeaten egg whites), fold in stiff-beaten egg whites.

Whip cream just till soft peaks form; fold into berry mixture. Chill till mixture mounds. Pile into pastry shell. Chill for 8 hours or till firm. If desired, garnish with additional berries and additional whipped cream.

Cherries

Selecting: *Look for cherries that are full-colored, firm, and plump. Stems should be fresh with a green cast. Avoid cherries that are soft, shriveled, sticky, or leaky. Color and size depend on variety. Pictured from top to bottom are Royal Ann, Montmorency, and Bing varieties. The Royal Ann cherries are large and sweet, amber to yellow in color with a delicate red blush. The Montmorency variety, which is the most common variety of tart red cherries, ranges in color from light to dark red. The Bing variety, the most popular of all sweet cherries, is characterized by large size and deep mahogany color. Royal Ann and Montmorency varieties are rarely found fresh. The Royal Anns usually are canned; the Montmorency variety usually is canned or frozen. Bing cherries and the other sweet varieties are available fresh from May to August.*

Storing: *Store this fruit lightly covered in the refrigerator for several days. Be sure to rinse and sort before using.*

Serving: *Serve dark sweet cherries for snacks or in salads and desserts. Sweeten tart red cherries and use in desserts.*

Cherry-Wine Soup

- 1 16-ounce can pitted tart red cherries
- ½ cup sugar
- 1 tablespoon quick-cooking tapioca
- ⅛ teaspoon ground cloves
- ½ cup dry red wine

In medium saucepan stir together *undrained* cherries, sugar, tapioca, cloves, and 1½ cups *water*. Let stand for 5 minutes. Bring to boiling. Reduce heat; cover and simmer for 15 minutes, stirring occasionally. Remove from heat; stir in wine. Cover and chill thoroughly, stirring occasionally. Makes 6 to 8 servings.

Orange-Cherry Cake

- 8 egg yolks
- ⅔ cup sugar
- 1 teaspoon finely shredded orange peel
- ¼ cup orange juice
- 1 cup sifted cake flour
- 8 egg whites (1 cup)
- 1 teaspoon cream of tartar
- ⅔ cup sugar
- 2 cups whipping cream
- 2 tablespoons sugar
- 4 cups fresh dark sweet cherries, pitted

Beat egg yolks at high speed of electric mixer till thick and lemon-colored. Gradually add ⅔ cup sugar, beating till sugar dissolves. Combine orange peel and orange juice. Beat juice mixture and cake flour alternately into yolk mixture.

Beat egg whites with cream of tartar and ½ teaspoon *salt* till soft peaks form. Gradually add ⅔ cup sugar, beating till stiff peaks form. Pour yolk mixture in thin stream over egg whites; fold in. Pour into *ungreased* 10-inch tube pan. Bake in 325° oven for 60 to 70 minutes. Invert cake in pan; cool. Remove cake from pan; split into 3 layers. Quarter the cherries. Whip cream with 2 tablespoons sugar till stiff peaks form. If desired, fold in 2 tablespoons brandy. Assemble cake by alternating layers of cake, whipped cream, and cherries.

Rich yet airy, this *Orange-Cherry Cake* attests to the possibilities of fresh dark sweet cherries. When cherry season has passed, keep this idea in mind for fresh berries.

Cherry-Cheese Pizza Pie

1¾ cups all-purpose flour
½ cup butter *or* margarine
3 tablespoons shortening
1 beaten egg yolk
3 tablespoons ice cold water
1 8-ounce package cream
   cheese, softened
½ cup sugar
2 eggs
⅓ cup chopped walnuts
1 teaspoon vanilla
⅔ cup sugar
2 tablespoons cornstarch
½ cup cold water
3 cups fresh *or* frozen pitted
   tart red cherries, thawed
   (16 ounces)
1 tablespoon butter *or* margarine
   Few drops almond extract
   Few drops red food coloring
   (optional)
   Whipped cream

Combine flour and ¾ teaspoon *salt*; cut in ½ cup butter or margarine and shortening till pieces are the size of fine crumbs. Combine egg yolk and 3 tablespoons ice cold water; gradually add to flour mixture and mix well. Using fingers, gently knead to form a ball. Cover; chill for 30 to 60 minutes. Roll pastry into a 13-inch circle. Line a 12-inch pizza pan. Trim pastry to ½ inch beyond edge of pan. Flute edge; prick pastry. Bake in 350° oven for 15 minutes. Cool.

In small mixer bowl combine cream cheese and ½ cup sugar; beat till fluffy. Beat in eggs. Stir in walnuts and vanilla. Pour cheese mixture into crust. Bake in 350° oven for 12 to 15 minutes or till set. Cool.

In saucepan combine ⅔ cup sugar, cornstarch, and dash *salt*. Stir in ½ cup cold water; cook and stir till thickened and bubbly. Stir in cherries, 1 tablespoon butter or margarine, and almond extract. If desired, stir in food coloring. Spread cherry mixture over cheese layer. Chill. To serve, garnish with whipped cream.

Sweet Cherry Bombe

2 cups fresh *or* frozen pitted
   dark sweet cherries, thawed
   and finely chopped
   (10 ounces)
1 14-ounce can (1¼ cups)
   sweetened condensed milk
1 teaspoon vanilla
   Few drops almond extract
1 cup whipping cream
   Few drops red food coloring
   (optional)
1 pint chocolate-nut ice cream

Combine cherries, condensed milk, vanilla, and almond extract. Pour into an 8x8x2-inch pan; freeze firm. Chill a 5-cup mold in freezer. Break up cherry mixture into chilled small mixer bowl; beat till fluffy. Whip cream just till soft peaks form; fold into cherry mixture. If desired, stir in food coloring. Remove *1 cup* cherry mixture; cover and freeze. Turn remaining cherry mixture into chilled mold; freeze slightly. Quickly spread over bottom and up sides of mold, leaving center hollow. (If mixture slips, refreeze till workable.) Stir chocolate-nut ice cream just to soften; spoon into center of mold, smoothing top. Spread the reserved cherry mixture over. Cover and freeze for 6 hours or overnight. Invert mold onto chilled plate. Rub mold with hot damp towel; lift off mold. Let stand at room temperature for 10 minutes. Makes 8 servings.

Cherries Jubilee

1 16-ounce can pitted dark sweet
   cherries
¼ cup sugar
2 tablespoons cornstarch
¼ cup brandy, cherry brandy,
   or Kirsch
   Vanilla ice cream

Drain cherries, reserving syrup. If necessary, add enough cold water to syrup to measure 1 cup liquid. In medium saucepan combine sugar and cornstarch; stir in the 1 cup liquid. Cook and stir till thickened and bubbly. Stir in cherries. Turn mixture into heat-proof bowl or blazer pan of chafing dish. Set over hot water.

Heat brandy or Kirsch in large ladle or small saucepan till it *almost* simmers. Ignite brandy and pour over cherry mixture. Stir to blend brandy into sauce. Serve immediately over ice cream. Makes 6 to 8 servings.

Cranberries

Selecting: Shop for fresh cranberries that are firm, plump, red, and glossy, even though size, shape, and color depend somewhat on the variety. Avoid purchasing any that appear to be dull, soft, sticky, or shriveled—indications of poor quality. The peak season for fresh cranberries runs from mid-September through December.

Storing: Refrigerate in the original package or loosely covered for up to two months. During the peak months, purchase extra to freeze for year-round use. Simply place the unopened package in the freezer. Cranberries may be stored in the freezer for up to a year. Rinse and sort both fresh and frozen cranberries just before using them. You need not thaw frozen cranberries before cooking with them.

Serving: Cranberries, one of only three native American fruits—Concord grapes and blueberries are the others—are perennial holiday favorites. But don't restrict them to the customary holiday sauce. Enjoy their tart flavor any time of the year in beverages, salads, main dishes, breads, and desserts. Canned and frozen cranberry products are available year-round and offer convenient shortcuts to many recipes. When coupled with other fruits, cranberries also can make attractive garnishes.

Cranberry-Spice Punch

- ¼ cup sugar
- 4 inches stick cinnamon
- ½ teaspoon whole cloves
- 2 32-ounce bottles cranberry juice cocktail, chilled
- 1 6-ounce can frozen limeade concentrate
- 1 6-ounce can frozen orange juice concentrate

In small saucepan combine sugar, cinnamon, cloves, and 1 cup *water*. Bring to boiling; reduce heat. Cover and simmer for 10 minutes. With slotted spoon remove spices. Cover and chill spiced liquid. To serve, in punch bowl combine spiced liquid, cranberry juice cocktail, frozen concentrates, and 3 cups *water*. Stir to dissolve frozen concentrates. If desired, float ice ring in punch bowl. *Or*, serve punch in glasses over cracked ice. Makes 28 (4-ounce) servings.

Cranberry-Orange Relish (pictured on page 4)

- 2 medium oranges
- 1 pound fresh *or* frozen cranberries
- 2 cups sugar
- ¼ cup finely chopped walnuts

With vegetable peeler remove orange portion of peel of one orange; reserve. Completely peel and section both oranges. Using food processor or coarse blade of food grinder, grind reserved orange peel, orange sections, and cranberries. Stir in sugar and walnuts. Cover and chill. If desired, serve in orange cups with sawtooth-cut edges. Makes 4 cups.

Cranberry Cheese Squares

1 envelope unflavored gelatin
1 cup ginger ale, chilled
1 16-ounce can whole cranberry
   sauce
2 tablespoons lemon juice
¼ teaspoon ground allspice
⅛ teaspoon ground nutmeg
1 11-ounce can mandarin orange
   sections, drained
1 3-ounce package raspberry-
   flavored gelatin
1 cup boiling water
1 3-ounce package cream
   cheese, softened
1 cup cranberry juice cocktail
½ cup whipping cream

In small saucepan soften unflavored gelatin in ½ *cup* of the ginger ale; heat and stir till gelatin dissolves. In medium bowl combine cranberry sauce, lemon juice, allspice, nutmeg, and remaining ginger ale; stir in gelatin mixture. Pour into an 8x8x2-inch pan. Arrange drained mandarin orange sections in cranberry sauce layer; chill till almost firm.

Meanwhile, dissolve raspberry gelatin in boiling water. In small mixer bowl blend raspberry gelatin mixture into cream cheese; beat till smooth. Stir in cranberry juice cocktail. Chill till partially set (consistency of unbeaten egg whites). Whip cream just till soft peaks form; fold into raspberry mixture. Pour over cranberry sauce layer. Chill for several hours or overnight or till firm. To serve, cut into squares. Makes 9 servings.

Cranberry-Burgundy Ham

1 5- to 7-pound cooked ham
   rump (butt) portion
   Whole cloves
1 16-ounce can whole cranberry
   sauce
½ cup packed brown sugar
½ cup burgundy
2 teaspoons prepared mustard

Score ham using a sharp knife to make shallow cuts diagonally across fat surface in diamond pattern. Stud with cloves. Place ham on rack in shallow baking pan. Insert meat thermometer. Bake, uncovered, in 325° oven for 1¼ to 1¾ hours.

Meanwhile, for glaze, in medium saucepan combine cranberry sauce, brown sugar, burgundy, and mustard. Heat and stir about 5 minutes or till sugar dissolves. Spoon about *half* of the glaze over ham and continue baking for 20 to 30 minutes longer or till meat thermometer registers 140°. Serve remaining glaze warm with ham. Makes 12 to 16 servings.

Cranberry-Stuffed Cornish Hens (pictured on page 4)

⅔ cup chopped cranberries
2 tablespoons sugar
1 teaspoon finely shredded
   orange peel
½ teaspoon salt
⅛ teaspoon ground cinnamon
4 slices raisin bread, toasted and
   cut into ½-inch cubes
   (3 cups)
2 tablespoons butter *or*
   margarine, melted
4 teaspoons orange juice
4 1- to 1½-pound Cornish game
   hens
   Salt
   Cooking oil
¼ cup orange juice
2 tablespoons butter *or*
   margarine, melted

In large bowl combine chopped cranberries, sugar, orange peel, ½ teaspoon salt, and cinnamon. Add raisin bread cubes; sprinkle with 2 tablespoons melted butter or margarine and 4 teaspoons orange juice. Gently toss.

Sprinkle cavities of hens with salt. Lightly stuff birds with cranberry mixture. Skewer neck skin to back of each bird. Tie legs to tail; twist wing tips under back. Place Cornish hens, breast side up, on rack in shallow baking pan. Brush with cooking oil; cover loosely with foil. Bake in 375° oven for 30 minutes.

Combine ¼ cup orange juice and 2 tablespoons melted butter or margarine. Uncover birds; baste with orange juice-butter mixture. Bake, uncovered, about 1 hour longer or till legs move easily in sockets, basting once or twice with orange juice-butter mixture. If desired, serve with Cranberry-Orange Relish (see recipe, page 39) and garnish with parsley and orange slices. Makes 4 servings.

Dates

Selecting: Sometimes called the candy that grows on trees, dates are usually classified as soft, semi-dry, or dry. Nonperishable dry varieties contain very little moisture when ripe. Semi-dry varieties are sold in their natural state as fresh dates, while the soft varieties are often dehydrated to bring them to the desired moisture level. Size, shape, and color of dates depend on variety. Pictured from top to bottom are: Royal Medjool, Zahidi, Deglet Noor, and Honey Ball Barhi date varieties. Noted for its large size, the Royal Medjool is a soft variety. The Zahidi date, fairly popular in the United States is a semi-dry variety, as is the Deglet Noor, the most common domestic date variety. The Honey Ball Barhi is a soft date. Dates may be purchased pitted, unpitted, or chopped. The season peaks in November, but dates are available year round.

Storing: Store them in the refrigerator. Because dates absorb moisture and odor easily, keep them tightly covered.

Serving: To pit dates, cut a lengthwise slit and use the knife tip to remove the pit. When snipping or chopping dates, dip shears or knife in cold water. Eat dates right from the package as a confection or sprinkle them over cereal or fruit salads. Add them to breads, muffins, coffee cakes, cookies, cakes, and pies.

Date-Nut Cake Roll

1 cup pitted whole dates, snipped
1 cup water
¼ cup granulated sugar
⅛ teaspoon salt
3 eggs
½ cup granulated sugar
1 cup all-purpose flour
1 teaspoon baking powder
½ teaspoon salt
½ teaspoon ground allspice
¾ cup chopped walnuts
  Powdered sugar
  Cream Cheese Filling

In small saucepan combine dates, water, ¼ cup granulated sugar, and ⅛ teaspoon salt. Bring to boiling. Cook and stir over low heat about 4 minutes or till thick. Remove from heat; cool to room temperature.

In small mixer bowl beat eggs at high speed of electric mixer for 5 minutes or till thick and lemon-colored. Gradually beat in ½ cup granulated sugar. Stir in date mixture. Stir together flour, baking powder, ½ teaspoon salt, and allspice. Fold flour mixture into egg mixture. Spread batter into greased and floured 15x10x1-inch jelly roll pan. Sprinkle with walnuts. Bake in 375° oven for 12 to 15 minutes. Turn out onto towel sprinkled with a little powdered sugar. Starting at narrow end, roll up cake with towel; cool. Unroll cake; spread evenly with Cream Cheese Filling. Reroll cake without towel; chill. Makes 10 servings.

Cream Cheese Filling: In small mixer bowl combine two 3-ounce packages *cream cheese*, ¼ cup *butter or margarine*, and ½ teaspoon *vanilla*. Beat till smooth. Beat in 1 cup sifted *powdered sugar*.

Grapefruit

Selecting: *Choose those that are well-rounded and heavy for their size, with a thin, smooth, fine-textured skin. Thin-skinned fruits contain more juice than those with thick skin. Minor scars or surface discolorations do not affect flavor or quality, but bad bruises may indicate damage to the interior. Color can range from pale yellow to russet or bronze and is not always a good indication of flavor or ripeness. Pulp of the fruit can be white or pink, with a range of color intensities between. The grapefruit is available throughout the year with peak availability from November through April.*

Storing: *Store them uncovered in the crisper section of the refrigerator. Kept in this way they will stay fresh for one to two weeks.*

Serving: *Grapefruit halves may be served for breakfast, as a first course, or as a dessert. For something different, serve broiled grapefruit halves. To prepare, cut a thin slice from the bottom of each half to balance grapefruit. Cut around each section close to the membrane; fruit should be completely loosened from shell. Remove core from each half; dot with butter. Sprinkle with brown sugar and ground cinnamon. Broil 4 inches from heat for 8 minutes; serve each topped with a maraschino cherry. Grapefruit sections add a tart, citrus flavor to salads and desserts. Use grapefruit juice in beverages, or as an ingredient in molded salads and desserts.*

Grapefruit Chiffon Cake

2¼ cups sifted cake flour
1½ cups sugar
1 tablespoon baking powder
1 teaspoon salt
½ cup cooking oil
5 egg yolks
1 tablespoon finely shredded grapefruit peel
⅔ cup grapefruit juice
8 egg whites (1 cup)
½ teaspoon cream of tartar
Cream Cheese Frosting

In a small mixer bowl sift together flour, sugar, baking powder, and salt; make a well in center. Add oil, egg yolks, grapefruit peel, and juice. Beat at low speed of electric mixer till combined, then at high speed for 5 minutes or till smooth. In large mixer bowl beat egg whites and cream of tartar till *very stiff* peaks form. Pour flour mixture in thin stream over surface of egg whites; fold in gently. Pour into *ungreased* 10-inch tube pan. Bake in 325° oven about 70 minutes or till cake tests done. Invert cake in pan; cool. Remove cake from pan. Spread Cream Cheese Frosting on top; drizzle down sides of cake. Chill.

Cream Cheese Frosting: Cream one 3-ounce package *cream cheese*, softened, with 1 cup sifted *powdered sugar* till fluffy. Beat in 1 tablespoon finely shredded *grapefruit peel* and ½ teaspoon *vanilla*. Add enough *grapefruit juice* (1 to 2 teaspoons) to make of spreading consistency.

Grapes

Selecting: When selecting grapes look for well-colored, plump fruit. Berries should be firmly attached to green pliable stems. Color is a good indication of ripeness, because grapes do not ripen after harvesting. White (green) grapes have an amber coloring when mature. Red varieties should be predominantly red. Darker varieties should have a rich color and be free of any green tinge. Table grapes are grouped as European (Western) and American (Eastern) varieties. Important European varieties are: Thompson Seedless, Emperor, Exotic, Cardinal, Tokay, Lady Finger, Almeria, Calmeria, and Perlette. Popular American varieties are: Concord, Niagara, Delaware, and Catawba. Varieties shown here, clockwise from top, are: Exotic, Cardinal, Concord, and Thompson Seedless. Grapes are available year round with peak availability from July through November.

Storing: Grapes are highly perishable. Store them unwashed and uncovered in the crisper of the refrigerator; use within three to five days.

Serving: Wash grapes before using. Use kitchen shears to halve them and to snip out the seeds. Serve as is for snacks, or use in salads and desserts, and in main dish accompaniments. Grapes also make an excellent garnish.

Purple Cows

1 pint vanilla ice cream
½ cup milk
⅓ cup frozen grape juice
   concentrate
2 tablespoons frozen lemonade
   concentrate

In blender container combine ice cream, milk, and frozen juice concentrates. Cover and blend till smooth. Serve in tall glasses with straws. If desired, garnish with whipped dessert topping and mint leaves. Makes 2 or 3 servings.

Elegant Turkey Salad

1 cup seedless green grapes
2 cups cubed cooked turkey
½ cup sliced celery
3 tablespoons sliced green onion
   Sour Cream Dressing

Halve grapes; combine with turkey, celery, and onion. Cover and chill. Toss with Sour Cream Dressing. If desired, stir in ½ cup toasted slivered *almonds*. Makes 4 to 6 servings.

Sour Cream Dressing: Combine ½ cup dairy *sour cream* and ¼ cup *mayonnaise*; mix well.

Halibut Veronique (pictured on page 16)

4 fresh *or* frozen halibut steaks
½ cup dry white wine
5 teaspoons cornstarch
1 tablespoon sliced green onion
2 teaspoons instant chicken
   bouillon granules
1 cup seedless green grapes
1 tablespoon snipped parsley
1 tablespoon butter *or* margarine
1 teaspoon lemon juice

Thaw fish, if frozen. Place steaks in greased skillet. Add water to cover. Bring to boiling; reduce heat. Cover and simmer 8 to 10 minutes or till fish flakes easily with a fork. Remove halibut to platter; keep warm. Meanwhile, in small saucepan combine wine, cornstarch, and ¾ cup *cold water*; stir in green onion and bouillon granules. Cook and stir till bubbly. Stir in grapes, parsley, butter, and lemon juice; heat through. To serve, spoon sauce over fish. If desired, garnish with lemon slices and parsley. Makes 4 servings.

Fruited Chicken Breasts

¼ teaspoon finely shredded
   orange peel
½ cup orange juice
1 tablespoon chopped onion
1 teaspoon instant chicken
   bouillon granules
3 whole medium chicken breasts
   Paprika
1 tablespoon cornstarch
½ cup seedless green grapes,
   halved

In skillet combine orange peel, orange juice, onion, and bouillon granules. Skin chicken breasts; halve lengthwise. Place chicken in skillet. Sprinkle with paprika and a little salt and pepper. Cover and simmer for 30 to 35 minutes or till chicken is tender. Remove chicken to platter; keep warm. Measure pan juices; add water, if necessary, to make ¾ cup liquid. Return to pan. Blend 1 tablespoon *cold water* into cornstarch; stir into reserved liquid. Cook and stir till bubbly. Add grapes; cook and stir 2 minutes more. Spoon some sauce over chicken; pass remainder. Makes 6 servings.

Concord Grape Pie

Pastry for Single-Crust Pie
   (see recipe page 22)
1½ pounds Concord grapes
   (4 cups)
¾ cup sugar
⅓ cup all-purpose flour
¼ teaspoon salt
2 tablespoons butter *or*
   margarine, melted
1 tablespoon lemon juice
½ cup all-purpose flour
½ cup sugar
¼ cup butter *or* margarine

Prepare and roll out pastry into a 12-inch circle. Line a 9-inch pie plate. Flute edge; do not prick pastry. Slip skins from grapes; set skins aside. In saucepan bring grape pulp to boiling; reduce heat and simmer 5 minutes. Sieve to remove seeds. Add skins to pulp. Combine ¾ cup sugar, ⅓ cup flour, and the salt. Stir in the melted butter or margarine, lemon juice, and grape mixture. Pour into pastry shell. To prevent overbrowning, cover edge of pie with foil. Bake in 375° oven for 20 to 25 minutes.

Meanwhile, combine ½ cup flour and ½ cup sugar. Cut in ¼ cup butter till crumbly. Remove foil from pie. Sprinkle crumb mixture over pie. Bake about 25 minutes more or till topping is golden. Cool.

Grape-Nectarine Compote

6 medium nectarines
3 cups seedless green grapes
1 cup white grape juice
2 tablespoons orange liqueur
2 tablespoons honey
1 pint lemon sherbert

Halve, pit, and slice nectarines. In large bowl combine nectarines and grapes. Add grape juice, orange liqueur, and honey; stir gently. Cover and chill. To serve, spoon fruit mixture into sherbet dishes; top each serving with a scoop of sherbet. Makes 8 to 10 servings.

Lemons & Limes

Selecting: When selecting these two fruits, look for rich color, a glossy, fine-textured skin, and those that are heavy for their size. There are two main categories of lemons and limes—acid and sweet. The acid type is the most prevalent in the United States. Although they are available year round, supplies of lemons and limes are most plentiful during the months of June, July, and August.

Storing: Both fruits will remain fresh for several weeks in the refrigerator. Lemons keep well in the crisper section, but limes should not be stored there because of the high humidity. Store limes in a dry place in the refrigerator.

Serving: The juice and peel of lemons and limes are flavor enhancers for beverages, breads, main dishes, and vegetables. They also can be the main flavor emphasis in a variety of salads and desserts. For colorful garnishes, make cartwheels by cutting V-shaped notches around the edges of the fruit slices or cut strips of peel and shape in a spiral fashion.

Orange Lemonade (pictured on the cover)

1¾ cups sugar
2½ cups water
8 lemons
4 to 5 oranges
1 sprig fresh mint (optional)
Ice cubes
Water
Lemon slices (optional)

In medium saucepan combine sugar and water. Cook over medium heat till sugar dissolves, stirring occasionally. Cool.

Finely shred enough lemon and orange peel to make 2 tablespoons; set aside. Squeeze juice from the lemons and oranges; you should have about 1½ cups lemon juice and 1½ cups orange juice. Add juices and peel to cooled syrup. If desired, pour over mint sprig. Cover and let stand for 1 hour. Strain mixture. Pour into jars; cover and refrigerate. To serve, fill glasses or pitcher with ice cubes. Pour equal parts of water and fruit syrup over ice; stir to combine. If desired, garnish with lemon slices. Makes 6 cups fruit syrup or 12 (8-ounce) servings of orange lemonade.

Frozen Daiquiri

1 6-ounce can frozen limeade concentrate
1 6-ounce can frozen lemonade concentrate
1 juice can (¾ cup) light rum
1 juice can (¾ cup) water
1 16-ounce bottle lemon-lime carbonated beverage
Lime slices (optional)

Combine limeade concentrate, lemonade concentrate, rum, and water; gently stir in carbonated beverage. Pour into 9x9x2-inch pan. Freeze till firm. To serve, spoon mixture into cocktail glasses. If desired, garnish each serving with a lime slice. Keep remaining mixture in covered container in freezer. Makes about 5 cups.

Kiwi Lime Layer Pie

¾ **cup sugar**
⅓ **cup all-purpose flour**
⅛ **teaspoon salt**
1¾ **cups milk**
3 **slightly beaten eggs**
¼ **cup butter** *or* **margarine**
2 **teaspoons finely shredded lime peel**
¼ **cup lime juice**
1 **8-ounce carton (1 cup) lemon yogurt**
 Few drops green food coloring (optional)
 Pastry
3 **tablespoons apple jelly**
 Whipped cream
 Kiwi fruit, peeled and sliced
 Lime slices

In saucepan combine sugar, flour, and salt; stir in milk. Cook and stir till bubbly. Cook and stir 2 minutes more. Stir *1 cup* of the hot mixture into eggs. Return all to saucepan. Cook and stir till bubbly; cook and stir 2 minutes more. Remove from heat. Stir in butter, peel, and juice. Fold in yogurt. If desired, add food coloring. Cool.

Prepare Pastry; divide in half. Roll out half; line a 9-inch pie plate. Trim ½ inch beyond edge. Flute; prick. Bake in 450° oven for 10 to 12 minutes. Cool. Divide remaining pastry in half; roll out each half to ⅛-inch thickness. Trim one to an 8-inch circle and one to an 8¾-inch circle. Place on baking sheet; prick. Bake in 450° oven for 8 to 10 minutes. Cool. To assemble, brush baked pastry shell with *1 tablespoon* jelly. Place *1 cup* filling in pastry shell; top with 8-inch pastry circle. Brush with *1 tablespoon* jelly. Repeat with *1¼ cups* filling and the 8¾-inch circle. Brush with remaining jelly. Top with remaining filling. Cover; chill. Pipe whipped cream around edge; arrange kiwi fruit slices and lime slices atop.

Pastry: In mixing bowl combine 2 cups all-purpose *flour* and 1 teaspoon *salt*. Cut in ⅔ cup *shortening or lard* till pieces are the size of small peas. Sprinkle 1 tablespoon cold *water* over part of mixture; gently toss with a fork. Push to side of bowl. Repeat, using a total of 6 to 7 tablespoons cold *water*, till all is moistened.

Strawberry-Filled Lemon Ring

1 **3-ounce package cream cheese**
1 **3-ounce package lemon-flavored gelatin**
1 **egg yolk**
½ **cup dairy sour cream**
¼ **teaspoon finely shredded lemon peel**
1 **tablespoon lemon juice**
1 **stiff-beaten egg white**
1 **cup fresh** *or* **frozen unsweetened strawberries**

Soften cream cheese. Dissolve gelatin in 1¼ cups *boiling water*; cool to room temperature. In a large bowl thoroughly combine cream cheese, egg yolk, and ⅛ teaspoon *salt*. Stir in sour cream, lemon peel, and lemon juice. Stir cooled gelatin mixture into sour cream mixture. Chill till partially set (consistency of unbeaten egg whites). Gently fold in the beaten egg white; slice strawberries; fold in. Turn into a 3½-cup ring mold. Chill several hours or till firm. Unmold gelatin on lettuce-lined platter. If desired, fill center of ring with whole strawberries. Makes 4 or 5 servings.

Lemon Chicken and Mushroom Broil

1 **2½- to 3-pound broiler-fryer chicken, quartered**
2 **cups whole fresh mushrooms**
⅓ **cup lemon juice**
¼ **cup cooking oil**
1 **clove garlic, minced**
¾ **teaspoon ground nutmeg**
½ **teaspoon salt**
⅛ **teaspoon pepper**

Place chicken and mushrooms in a plastic bag; set in shallow pan. For marinade, combine remaining ingredients. Pour over chicken and mushrooms; close bag. Marinate about 30 minutes at room temperature; turn often. Drain; reserve marinade. Place chicken, skin side down, on rack of unheated broiler pan. Broil 6 inches from heat about 20 minutes. Brush often with marinade. Turn chicken skin side up; broil 15 to 20 minutes more or till tender, adding mushrooms the last 10 minutes of broiling. Brush occasionally with marinade. Makes 4 servings.

Creamy lime filling and flaky pastry are topped with slices of kiwi fruit in
Kiwi Lime Layer Pie. Swirls of whipped cream and lime slices garnish this tempting dessert.

Glazed Lime Loaf

1 beaten egg
1½ cups milk
¼ cup cooking oil
2 teaspoons finely shredded lime peel
¼ cup lime juice
3 cups all-purpose flour
1 cup sugar
1 tablespoon baking powder
¼ teaspoon baking soda
2 tablespoons lime juice

In a small mixing bowl combine egg, milk, oil, lime peel, and ¼ cup lime juice. In large mixing bowl stir together flour, ¾ *cup* of the sugar, the baking powder, baking soda, and 1 teaspoon *salt*. Make a well in the center. Add egg mixture all at once. Stir just till moistened (batter should be lumpy). Turn batter into greased 9x5x3-inch loaf pan. Bake in 350° oven for 1 hour. Cool in pan 10 minutes; remove from pan onto wire rack. Prick holes in hot loaf with a fork. In saucepan combine remaining ¼ cup sugar and the 2 tablespoons lime juice; heat just till sugar dissolves. Spoon over top of hot loaf. Cool completely. Makes 1 loaf.

Individual Lemon Soufflés

4 slightly beaten egg yolks
¼ cup granulated sugar
¼ cup butter *or* margarine
½ teaspoon finely shredded lemon peel
¼ cup lemon juice
4 egg whites
¼ cup granulated sugar

Combine egg yolks, ¼ cup sugar, butter, peel, juice, and dash *salt*. Cook and stir till thickened. Remove from heat; beat 2 minutes. Beat egg whites to soft peaks. Gradually add ¼ cup sugar; beat to stiff peaks. Fold yolk mixture into egg whites. Spoon into four individual soufflé dishes. Place in shallow baking pan; pour hot water into pan to depth of ½ inch. Bake in 350° oven 30 to 35 minutes. If desired, sprinkle with powdered sugar. Serve immediately. Serves 4.

Lemon Meringue Pie

Pastry for Single-Crust Pie (see recipe, page 22)
1½ cups sugar
3 tablespoons cornstarch
3 tablespoons all-purpose flour
3 slightly beaten egg yolks
2 tablespoons butter *or* margarine
½ teaspoon finely shredded lemon peel
⅓ cup lemon juice
3 egg whites
½ teaspoon vanilla
¼ teaspoon cream of tartar
6 tablespoons sugar

Prepare and roll out pastry into a 12-inch circle. Transfer to a 9-inch pie plate. Flute edge; prick pastry. Bake in 450° oven for 10 to 12 minutes. Cool. Combine 1½ cups sugar, the cornstarch, flour, and dash *salt*. Stir in 1½ cups *water*. Cook and stir till thickened and bubbly. Cook and stir 2 minutes more. Remove from heat. Stir *1 cup* of the hot mixture into the yolks. Return all to saucepan. Bring to gentle boil. Cook and stir 2 minutes more. Remove from heat. Add butter and lemon peel. Stir in lemon juice. Turn into pastry shell. For meringue, beat egg whites with vanilla and cream of tartar till soft peaks form. Gradually add the 6 tablespoons sugar, beating till stiff peaks form. Spread over hot filling. Bake in 350° oven for 12 to 15 minutes or till golden. Cool; refrigerate.

Lemon Pudding Cake

¾ cup sugar
¼ cup all-purpose flour
3 tablespoons butter, melted
1½ teaspoons grated lemon peel
¼ cup lemon juice
3 beaten egg yolks
1½ cups milk
3 egg whites

Combine sugar, flour, and a dash *salt*. Stir in butter, lemon peel, and lemon juice. Combine egg yolks and milk; add to flour mixture. Beat egg whites till stiff peaks form; fold in egg whites. Turn into ungreased 8x8x2-inch baking pan. Place in larger pan on oven rack. Pour hot water into larger pan to depth of 1 inch. Bake in 350° oven for 35 to 40 minutes or till top is golden and springs back when touched. Serve warm or chilled. Makes 6 to 8 servings.

Melons

Selection: Color of the rind, aroma, and the condition of the blossom end are the key guides to melon quality. Cantaloupes should have a raised, netted rind with a golden background, and a smooth, rounded scar at the stem end. Look for well-shaped watermelons with a yellowish underside and a dull rather than shiny surface. Cantaloupes should be vine-ripened, as should watermelons. Melons that will ripen at room temperature are the honeydew, honeyball, casaba, crenshaw and Persian. With the exception of watermelon and casaba, melons have a pleasant, fruity aroma when ready to eat. Melons shown here are, clockwise front to back: cantaloupe, honeydew, watermelon, crenshaw, Persian, and casaba. Melons are plentiful during the summer and early fall, with the exception of watermelons, which are most abundant from late spring through the summer.

Storing: Place ripened melons in a plastic bag or wrap in foil; refrigerate. Store away from lettuce, carrots, celery, broccoli, butter, or other dairy products because these foods can absorb melon aroma. Use within three to five days.

Serving: Serve chilled melon halves or wedges as a nutritious snack or as part of a meal. Melon balls can be served as an appetizer, and they make a colorful addition to fruit cups, salads, and desserts.

Orange Melon Frost

2 **cups desired melon pieces**★
¼ **cup dairy sour cream**
¼ **cup milk**
1 **tablespoon sugar**
1 **cup orange** *or* **lemon sherbet**

In blender container combine melon pieces, sour cream, milk, and sugar. Cover; blend till smooth. Add sherbet; cover and blend till smooth. Pour into 4 chilled glasses. If desired, garnish with melon balls. Makes 4 servings.

★Cantaloupe, honeydew, casaba, crenshaw, or Persian melon.

Prosciutto and Melon Appetizers

1 **cantaloupe, honeydew, casaba, crenshaw,** *or* **Persian melon**
4 **ounces thinly sliced prosciutto**
8 **ounces Swiss cheese**
　 Leaf lettuce

Halve and seed melon; scoop out melon balls. Scrape any remaining fruit from shell. Cut prosciutto into 1-inch-wide strips; cut cheese into ¾-inch cubes. On wooden picks thread melon, prosciutto, and cheese, threading prosciutto accordion style. Line melon shells with lettuce leaves; fill with appetizers. Makes about 30 appetizers.

Fresh Fruit Mixer with Watermelon Ice

1 **medium watermelon, well-chilled**
1 **medium pineapple, peeled, cored, and cubed (2 cups)**
3 **cups seedless green grapes, halved**
3 **medium nectarines, pitted and sliced**
4 **medium plums, pitted and sliced**
2 **cups blueberries**
Watermelon Ice

Cut thin slice off bottom of melon to make it sit flat. Slice off top one-fourth of melon. Carefully scoop out melon pulp and remove seeds; reserve pulp. Cut top edge of melon shell in scalloped fashion; cover shell and refrigerate. Prepare Watermelon Ice; cube any remaining melon pulp. Combine cubed melon, pineapple, grapes, nectarines, plums, and blueberries; turn into chilled watermelon shell. Just before serving, top fruit in shell with scoops of Watermelon Ice. (Or, serve Watermelon Ice atop individual servings of the fruit mixture.) Makes 12 to 14 servings.

Watermelon Ice: In blender container place about *2 cups* of the reserved melon pulp. Cover and blend till smooth. Measure and transfer to large bowl. Repeat with enough of the remaining melon to make *3 cups* puree. Stir in ¾ cup *sugar*, 3 tablespoons *lemon juice*, and dash *salt*.

In small saucepan soften 1 teaspoon *unflavored gelatin* in ¼ cup cold *water*. Heat and stir till gelatin dissolves. Add gelatin mixture to melon mixture; blend thoroughly. Pour mixture into 9x9x2-inch pan; cover and freeze till partially frozen. Turn mixture into chilled large mixer bowl. Beat at medium speed of electric mixer till light and fluffy. Return to pan. Freeze till firm. Let stand 5 minutes before scooping. Makes 4 cups ice.

Fruit-Filled Melon Bowls (pictured on page 16)

1 **3-ounce package cream cheese, softened**
⅔ **cup strawberry yogurt**
2 **small cantaloupe *or* honeydew melons**
2 **medium bananas**
2 **cups fresh strawberries, halved**
Leaf lettuce
Mint sprigs (optional)

In small mixer bowl beat cream cheese with electric mixer till fluffy. On low speed add *half* of the yogurt; beat till smooth. Stir in remaining yogurt by hand. Cover and chill.

Halve and seed melons; scoop out melon balls. Scrape any remaining fruit from shell (chill for another use). Reserve melon shells. Cut bananas into bias slices. Combine melon balls, bananas, and strawberries. Line melon shells with lettuce leaves; spoon fruit mixture into shells. Spoon yogurt mixture over fruit. If desired, garnish each with a sprig of mint. Makes 4 servings.

Honeydew Fruit Salad (pictured on the cover)

2 **small honeydew melons**
1 **cup fully cooked ham cut into julienne strips**
2 **large peaches, peeled, pitted, and sliced *or* chopped**
1 **cup seeded, halved red grapes *or* halved pitted dark sweet cherries**
¼ **cup chopped celery**
½ **cup peach yogurt**
1 **teaspoon sugar (optional)**

Cut melons into halves. Remove seeds. In large bowl combine ham, peaches, grapes, and celery. Toss to mix. Spoon fruit mixture into melon halves. In small bowl blend peach yogurt and sugar, if desired; spoon yogurt over fruit mixture. Makes 4 servings.

Fresh Fruit Mixer with Watermelon Ice uses frosty scoops of ice
made from watermelon pulp as a topper for this combination of fresh fruits.

Oranges & Tangerines

Selecting: *Choose firm, smooth-skinned oranges that are heavy for their size (a sign of juiciness). Color is not a reliable indication of ripeness. Varieties of oranges are divided into two groups, sweet and sour. Valencia and Navel, both sweet, are the dominant varieties. Tangerines are actually a type of mandarin orange. Smaller than oranges, they are flattened at both ends, and have a pebbly, easy-to-remove skin. Shown here, clockwise from top, are: Valencia, Tangelo, Satsuma Mandarin, Navel, and Tangerine. Oranges are available year-round. Tangerines are available from October through May, with peak supplies from November through January.*

Storing: *Refrigerate oranges or store at room temperature if they will be used within a few days. Refrigerate tangerines.*

Serving: *Oranges and tangerines are popular for use as snacks or in beverages, salads, breads, fruit cups, and desserts.*

Fruit Platter with Orange Dressing (pictured on page 4)

1 **slightly beaten egg**	In small saucepan combine egg, orange juice, honey, lemon juice, cardamom, and dash *salt*. Cook and stir over medium-low heat till mixture thickens. Cover; cool. Beat cream till soft peaks form. Fold into cooled egg mixture. Cover and chill. Arrange fruits on a platter. Serve with dressing. If desired, garnish dressing with shredded orange peel. Makes 1⅓ cups dressing.

1 **slightly beaten egg**
¼ **cup orange juice**
2 **tablespoons honey**
1 **tablespoon lemon juice**
½ **teaspoon ground cardamom**
½ **cup whipping cream**
  Assorted fresh fruits

In small saucepan combine egg, orange juice, honey, lemon juice, cardamom, and dash *salt*. Cook and stir over medium-low heat till mixture thickens. Cover; cool. Beat cream till soft peaks form. Fold into cooled egg mixture. Cover and chill. Arrange fruits on a platter. Serve with dressing. If desired, garnish dressing with shredded orange peel. Makes 1⅓ cups dressing.

Spiced Tangerine Mold

1 **cup tangerine *or* orange sections**
3 **inches stick cinnamon**
10 **whole cloves**
1 **3-ounce package lemon-flavored gelatin**
1 **cup orange juice**
1 **tablespoon lemon juice**
¼ **cup chopped walnuts**

Cut up tangerine or orange sections; set aside. In saucepan combine stick cinnamon, cloves, and 1 cup *water*. Bring to boiling. Reduce heat; cover and simmer for 5 minutes. Remove cinnamon and cloves. Add gelatin to saucepan, stirring till dissolved. Stir in orange and lemon juices. Chill till partially set. Fold in tangerine or orange pieces and nuts. Pour into 3½-cup mold. Chill till firm. Unmold onto lettuce-lined plate. Makes 4 to 6 servings.

Fresh Orange Coffee Ring

3 teaspoons finely shredded
   orange peel
2 medium oranges
   Milk
2½ to 3 cups all-purpose flour
1 package active dry yeast
¼ cup sugar
¼ cup shortening
½ teaspoon salt
1 egg
2 tablespoons butter or
   margarine, melted
2 tablespoons sugar
   Confectioners' Icing (see
   recipe, page 21)

Peel, section, and dice oranges over bowl to catch juice. Measure juice; add milk to make ¾ cup liquid (mixture will curdle). Set aside. In small mixer bowl combine *1 cup* of the flour, the yeast, and *1 teaspoon* of the orange peel. Heat milk mixture, ¼ cup sugar, shortening, and salt just till warm (115° to 120°); stir constantly. Add to flour mixture; stir in egg. Beat at low speed of electric mixer for 30 seconds, scraping sides of bowl. Beat 3 minutes at high speed. Stir in as much of the remaining flour as you can with a spoon. On a lightly floured surface, knead in enough of the remaining flour to make a moderately soft dough that is smooth and elastic (3 to 5 minutes total). Shape into a ball. Place in greased bowl; turn to grease surface. Cover; let rise in warm place till double (1 to 1½ hours). Punch down; cover and let rest 10 minutes. Roll dough to a 20x12-inch rectangle. Brush with melted butter or margarine. Combine 2 tablespoons sugar and the remaining orange peel; sprinkle over dough. Sprinkle orange pieces over dough. Roll up jelly-roll style, beginning at longest side; seal seams. Shape into ring on greased baking sheet, seam side down. With scissors snip ⅔ of the way to center at 1-inch intervals. Turn each section slightly to one side. Cover; let rise till almost double (about 30 minutes). Bake in 350° oven 20 to 25 minutes. Drizzle with Confectioners' Icing. Makes 1 coffee cake.

Orange Crepes

⅓ cup sugar
3 tablespoons all-purpose flour
½ teaspoon finely shredded
   orange peel
¼ teaspoon salt
1¼ cups milk
1 beaten egg
1 tablespoon butter or margarine
1 teaspoon vanilla
½ teaspoon finely shredded
   orange peel
1 cup orange juice
⅓ cup raisins
¼ cup sugar
   Crepes

For filling, combine ⅓ cup sugar, the flour, ½ teaspoon orange peel, and the salt. Blend in milk. Cook and stir till thickened and bubbly; cook and stir 2 minutes more. Gradually stir *half* of the hot mixture into beaten egg; return mixture to saucepan. Cook and stir just till bubbly. Remove from heat; stir in butter or margarine and vanilla. Cover surface with clear plastic wrap. Cool without stirring.

For sauce, combine ½ teaspoon orange peel, the orange juice, raisins, and ¼ cup sugar. Bring to boiling. Reduce heat. Cover; simmer 5 minutes. Set aside. Prepare crepes. Spread about *1 tablespoon* of the filling over unbrowned side of each crepe, leaving ¼-inch rim around edge. Roll up jelly-roll style. Place, seam side down, in greased 13x9x2-inch baking dish, forming 2 layers; pour sauce over. Cover; bake in 375° oven about 15 minutes. Makes 8 servings.

Crepes: Combine 1 cup all-purpose *flour*, 1½ cups *milk*, 2 *eggs*, 2 tablespoons *sugar*, 1 tablespoon *cooking oil*, and ⅛ teaspoon *salt*. Beat with rotary beater till blended. Heat a lightly greased 6-inch skillet. Remove from heat. Spoon in *2 tablespoons* batter; lift and tilt skillet to spread batter. Return to heat; brown on one side. Invert pan over paper toweling; remove crepes. Repeat to make 16 to 18 crepes, greasing skillet as needed.

Orange-Sauced Duckling

1   **4- to 5-pound domestic duckling**
Salt
Celery tops
1   **medium onion, quartered**
1   **medium orange**
1   **cup water**
1   **tablespoon sugar**
1   **tablespoon cornstarch**
1   **teaspoon instant chicken bouillon granules**
Dash ground ginger
2   **tablespoons vinegar**
1   **tablespoon orange liqueur (optional)**
Hot cooked brown rice (optional)
Parsley (optional)
Orange slices (optional)

Rinse duckling and pat dry. Season body cavity with a little salt and stuff with celery tops and quartered onion. Skewer neck skin to back. Tuck drumsticks under band of skin across tail or tie legs to tail. Twist wing tips under back. Place duckling, breast side up, on rack in shallow roasting pan. Prick skin all over to allow fat to escape. (Remove excess fat during roasting.) Roast, uncovered, in 375° oven for 1¾ to 2¼ hours or till drumstick moves easily in socket.

Meanwhile, cut peel from the orange. Remove white membrane from peel; slice peel into julienne strips. Section orange over bowl to catch juice. Add sections to juice; set aside. Simmer peel in 1 cup water for 15 minutes; drain well. If desired, reserve a few strips for garnish.

Remove duckling from pan; discard stuffing. Keep duckling warm. For sauce, skim fat from drippings. Add water to drippings to measure 1 cup liquid. Combine sugar, cornstarch, bouillon granules, and ginger. Blend in the 1 cup of drippings liquid and vinegar. Cook and stir till bubbly. Add reserved orange juice and sections, cooked peel, and orange liqueur. Cook and stir 2 minutes more. Serve sauce warm with roast duckling. If desired, serve duckling on bed of brown rice, garnished with reserved strips of peel, parsley, and orange slices. Makes 3 or 4 servings.

Italian Orange Flan (pictured on the cover)

1½   **cups all-purpose flour**
3   **tablespoons sugar**
5   **tablespoons butter *or* margarine, chilled**
1   **beaten egg**
2   **tablespoons cooking oil**
4   **teaspoons cold water**
⅓   **cup sugar**
2   **tablespoons cornstarch**
¼   **teaspoon salt**
1¼   **cups milk**
3   **beaten egg yolks**
3   **tablespoons brandy**
2   **cups fresh strawberries, halved**
3   **oranges, peeled and sectioned**
½   **cup orange marmalade**

For flan shell, in bowl stir together flour, 3 tablespoons sugar, and ½ teaspoon *salt*. Cut in butter or margarine till crumbly. Add beaten egg and oil; stir till flour mixture is moistened. Sprinkle water over mixture 1 teaspoon at a time, tossing with fork. Work mixture with hands till well blended. On lightly floured surface roll dough into a 13-inch circle. Fit dough into an 11-inch flan pan, pressing bottom and sides gently. Prick bottom; line with foil. Bake in 375° oven for 10 minutes; remove foil. Bake for 12 to 14 minutes more or till golden brown. Cool thoroughly on wire rack. Remove from pan; transfer flan shell to platter.

For custard filling, in heavy saucepan combine ⅓ cup sugar, cornstarch, and ¼ teaspoon salt; blend in milk. Cook and stir till thickened and bubbly. Cook and stir 2 minutes more. Gradually stir about *half* of the hot mixture into the beaten egg yolks; return to remaining hot mixture. Cook and stir till bubbly. Cook and stir 2 minutes more. Remove from heat. Stir in brandy. Cover surface with clear plastic wrap; cool thoroughly without stirring. Spread cooled mixture in bottom of flan shell; chill. About 1 to 1½ hours before serving, place strawberry halves around outer edge of flan atop custard filling, reserving 3 strawberry halves. Arrange orange sections spiral fashion in remaining area. Place reserved strawberry halves in center. Melt orange marmalade; spoon over fruit. Chill. Makes 8 to 10 servings.

Citrus adds a special flavor to succulent *Orange-Sauced Duckling*.
An orange sauce is a fitting complement to serve with this moist and tender bird.

Peaches & Nectarines

Selecting: Choose peaches that are firm to slightly soft with a yellow or creamy skin color. Nectarines should be firm, yet slightly soft along the "seam," with an orange-yellow color between red areas. The red "blush" of both is not a good indication of ripeness because it varies with the variety. Avoid very hard fruits because they will not ripen fully. Peaches and nectarines are classified as either freestone or clingstone. In the clingstone varieties, the flesh clings tightly to the stone, while the flesh of the freestone varieties is easily separated from the stone. The flesh of both types may be yellow or white. The yellow freestone varieties are the most popular of both peaches and nectarines. Both fruits are available from June through September, with peak availability during July and August.

Storing: Peaches and nectarines will ripen in two to three days at room temperature. When fully ripe, they should be kept uncovered in the refrigerator and used in a few days. Handle gently because both bruise easily.

Serving: As a snack, peaches and nectarines are best served at room temperature. For easy removal of the skin, place the fruits into boiling water for 20 to 30 seconds, then rinse with cold water. When cut or peeled, keep their color bright by treating with ascorbic acid color keeper or a citrus juice. Both fruits are excellent for use in beverages, salads, main dishes, pies, cakes, and other desserts, or as garnishes for meat or poultry.

Peach Fuzz

1 6-ounce can frozen pink
    lemonade concentrate
1 6-ounce juice can (¾ cup)
    vodka *or* light rum
1 10-ounce package frozen
    peach slices
¼ cup water
    Ice cubes
    Lemon slices (optional)
    Strawberry halves (optional)
    Mint leaves (optional)

In blender container combine juice concentrate, liquor, frozen peaches, and ¼ cup water; blend till smooth. Add ice cubes one at a time to make about 5 cups of slushy mixture. (If mixture becomes too thick before making 5 cups, add additional water.) Serve in chilled glasses with straws. If desired, garnish with lemon slices, strawberry halves, or mint leaves. Makes 4 to 6 servings.

Peachy Chicken Salad

1　12-ounce package frozen rice
　　pilaf
½　cup mayonnaise
¼　cup chopped green pepper
2　tablespoons sliced green
　　onion
½　teaspoon dried tarragon,
　　crushed
2　cups cubed cooked chicken
4　medium fresh peaches, peeled,
　　pitted, and sliced
　　Lettuce

Prepare rice pilaf according to package directions; cool in mixing bowl. Stir in mayonnaise, green pepper, green onion, and tarragon. Add chicken; toss lightly to coat. Cover and chill. Shortly before serving, add peaches and toss. Serve in lettuce cups. Makes 4 servings.

Beef and Peach Toss

⅓　cup salad oil
3　tablespoons vinegar
1　tablespoon prepared
　　horseradish
½　teaspoon salt
½　teaspoon worcestershire
　　sauce
⅛　teaspoon pepper
　　Few drops bottled hot pepper
　　sauce
3　cups thin strips or slices rare
　　roast beef or steak
1　head romaine, torn into bite-
　　size pieces (4 cups)
6　medium fresh peaches peeled,
　　pitted, and sliced or
　　one 29-ounce can peach
　　slices, drained
1　medium avocado, peeled,
　　seeded, and sliced
1　cup fresh strawberries, halved

For marinade, in screw-top jar combine oil, vinegar, horse-radish, salt, worcestershire sauce, pepper, and hot pepper sauce. In bowl sprinkle beef with a little salt and pepper; pour marinade over. Cover and refrigerate for several hours or overnight, stirring occasionally.

In salad bowl arrange romaine, peaches, avocado, and strawberries. Add *undrained* beef; toss lightly. Serves 6.

Glazed Corned Beef and Peaches

1　3-pound corned beef brisket
2　cups water
6　to 8 medium fresh peaches,
　　peeled, halved, and pitted or
　　one 29-ounce can peach
　　halves, drained
½　cup peach preserves
¼　teaspoon ground ginger

Rinse brisket in cold water to remove pickling juices. Place, fat side up, on rack in shallow roasting pan. Add water; cover with foil. Roast in 325° oven for 2 hours. Uncover; drain cooking liquid, reserving ½ cup liquid in pan. Arrange peach halves, cut side down, around corned beef in roasting pan. Return to oven; continue roasting, uncovered, for 30 minutes more.

For glaze, combine peach preserves and ginger. Turn peach halves cut side up. Spoon glaze over peaches and corned beef. Return to oven and roast for 10 to 15 minutes more or till glaze is heated through. Makes 6 to 8 servings.

Frozen Peaches and Cream Mousse

2 cups mashed fresh ripe peaches *or* two 10-ounce packages frozen peach slices, mashed
1 cup dairy sour cream
¼ cup sugar
3 tablespoons crème d'almond liqueur *or* peach brandy
1 quart vanilla ice cream
  Peach slices

Drain mashed peaches. Combine drained peaches, sour cream, sugar and liqueur *or* brandy. In large bowl stir ice cream just till softened; fold in peach mixture. Turn into 5-cup mold. Freeze several hours or overnight or till firm. Unmold onto serving plate. Let stand 15 minutes. If desired, drizzle with additional liqueur. Garnish with additional peach slices. Makes 8 to 10 servings.

Peaches Poached in Wine

1 cup sugar
1 cup dry red wine
4 whole cloves
2 inches stick cinnamon
1 teaspoon grated lemon peel
¼ cup lemon juice
6 firm ripe fresh peaches, peeled, pitted, and halved

In saucepan combine sugar and 1 cup *water*. Heat and stir to dissolve sugar. Remove from heat. Add wine, spices, lemon peel, and lemon juice. Place peaches in syrup mixture, turning to coat. Bring mixture to boiling; reduce heat. Cover and simmer about 5 minutes or till peaches are just tender. Turn peaches several times; cool in syrup. Chill. To serve, place 2 peach halves in each sherbet dish; pour about ⅓ cup syrup over each serving. Makes 6 servings.

Chilled Peach Soufflé

½ cup sugar
1 envelope unflavored gelatin
¼ teaspoon ground nutmeg
⅛ teaspoon salt
½ cup water
4 beaten egg yolks
1 tablespoon lemon juice
½ teaspoon vanilla
  Few drops almond extract
4 large fresh peaches
4 stiff-beaten egg whites
½ cup whipping cream
  Toasted sliced almonds (optional)

Combine sugar, gelatin, nutmeg, and salt. Stir in water. Cook and stir over low heat till gelatin dissolves. Gradually stir hot mixture into beaten egg yolks. Return to saucepan; add lemon juice. Cook and stir till thickened. Remove from heat. Stir in vanilla and almond extract. Peel, pit, and slice 2 of the peaches (about 1½ cups). Place sliced peaches in blender container. Cover; blend till finely chopped. Stir into gelatin mixture. Chill till partially set (consistency of unbeaten egg whites). Peel, pit and chop remaining peaches. Fold into gelatin mixture. Fold in the stiff-beaten egg whites. Whip cream; fold into gelatin. Chill till mixture mounds when dropped from a spoon. Turn into a 1½-quart soufflé dish. Chill till firm. If desired, garnish with toasted, sliced almonds and peaches. Makes 8 to 10 servings.

Nectarines Royale

1 cup sugar
8 medium nectarines, peeled, pitted, and quartered
¼ cup brandy
1½ teaspoons vanilla
⅛ teaspoon ground cinnamon
  Dash ground cloves
  Dairy sour cream

In 10-inch skillet combine sugar and 1 cup *water*; bring to boiling; add fruit. Return to boiling. Reduce heat and simmer, covered, about 5 minutes or till fruit is just tender. Remove from heat; stir in brandy, vanilla, and spices. Cool to room temperature; cover and chill. To serve, spoon fruit and syrup into dessert dishes; top with a dollop of sour cream. Makes 8 servings.

Peaches, ice cream, and sour cream team up in *Frozen Peaches and Cream Mousse*. Crème d'almond liqueur adds extra flavor and color to this easy-to-prepare dessert.

Pears

Selecting: Pears, unlike most other fruits, do not ripen well on the tree, so they must be picked unripe but mature. If picked when ripe, the fruit tends to be coarse, woody, and gritty. Pears are categorized according to the time of year they are harvested. Summer or early fall varieties are Bartlett and Seckel. Winter varieties include Anjou, Bosc, Comice and Winter Nelis. For all varieties, select firm pears that have just begun to soften. Ripeness is not indicated by color in winter varieties, because some may not change in color as they ripen. Bartlett and Seckel pears, however, do change color as they ripen. Bartletts have a clear yellow color when ripe. The red area on Seckel pears brightens and the green area becomes yellowish as ripening occurs. Pears may be purchased when firm and green and allowed to ripen for a few days at room temperature. When ripe, pears will yield to gentle pressure applied to the stem end. Pears are available year-round, but peak availability is from August through November. Pictured here, clockwise from back left, are: Red Bartlett, Anjou, Bosc, Comice, Bartlett, and Seckel.

Storing: Storage depends on the ripeness of the fruit. Allow underripe pears to stand at room temperature for a few days to ripen. Fully ripe pears should be refrigerated and used within a week.

Serving: Pears for "fresh" use, such as snacks, in salads, and with cheese, should be served fully ripe and chilled. Pears are excellent for use in desserts such as pies, crisps, and cookies. Those used for cooking and baking purposes are best when still firm and a bit underripe.

Minted Pear Mold

1 **3-ounce package lime-flavored gelatin**
2 **tablespoons crème de menthe syrup**
½ **cup dairy sour cream**
2 **cups cubed, peeled fresh pears** *or one 16-ounce can pear halves, drained and cubed*
Dairy sour cream (optional)

In large mixer bowl dissolve gelatin in 1 cup *boiling water*. Stir in ½ cup *cold water* and the crème de menthe syrup. Beat in ½ cup sour cream. Chill till partially set (consistency of unbeaten egg whites). Beat at high speed of electric mixer till light and fluffy; fold in pears. Turn into 4½-cup mold. Cover and chill several hours or overnight or till firm. If desired, serve with additional sour cream. Makes 6 to 8 servings.

Rosy Pear Compote

1   16-ounce can whole cranberry
      sauce
⅓ cup sugar
1   tablespoon lemon juice
¼ teaspoon ground cinnamon
¼ teaspoon ground ginger
6   medium fresh pears, peeled,
      cored, and quartered
2   oranges, peeled and sectioned

In medium saucepan combine cranberry sauce, sugar, lemon juice, cinnamon, and ginger. Bring to boiling. Place quartered pears and orange sections in 1½-quart casserole. Pour cranberry mixture over. Cover and bake in 350° oven for 35 minutes or till pears are tender. Spoon fruit mixture into individual sherbets or compotes. Serve warm. Makes 6 servings.

Ruby Wine Pears

1   3-ounce package strawberry-
      flavored gelatin
1   cup ruby port
6   inches stick cinnamon
6   whole cloves
6   fresh pears, peeled and cored

In 2-quart casserole combine gelatin and ¾ cup *boiling water*, stirring till gelatin is dissolved. Stir in port, cinnamon, and cloves. Add pears. Cover and bake in 350° oven for 50 minutes or till tender, turning pears several times. Serve warm or cold. If desired, top with whipping cream and sprinkle with ground nutmeg. Makes 6 servings.

Fresh Pear Dumplings

2   cups all-purpose flour
1   teaspoon salt
⅔ cup shortening *or* lard
6   to 7 tablespoons cold water
6   small pears, peeled and cored
1   3-ounce package cream
      cheese, softened
2   tablespoons chopped walnuts,
      toasted
6   teaspoons sugar
1¼ cups sugar
¼ cup red cinnamon candies
2   tablespoons butter *or*
      margarine

Stir together flour and salt. Cut in shortening till pieces are size of small peas. Sprinkle *1 tablespoon* water over part of mixture; gently toss. Push to side of bowl. Repeat till all is moistened. Form dough into ball. On lightly floured surface roll out into a 21x14-inch rectangle; cut into six 7-inch squares. Place one pear upright on center of *each* square. Blend cream cheese and nuts. Fill center of each pear with *1 tablespoon* cheese mixture; sprinkle with *1 teaspoon* sugar. Moisten edges of each pastry square. Fold corners of each square to center over pear; seal edges by pinching together. Place in 13x9x2-inch baking pan. Combine 1¼ cups sugar, candies, and 1½ cups *water*. Cook and stir till dissolved. Bring to boiling; add butter. Pour over dumplings. Bake in 400° oven for 35 to 40 minutes. Makes 6 servings.

Fresh Pear Crumble Pie

     Pastry for Single-Crust Pie
      (see recipe, page 22)
5   cups sliced, peeled, fresh
      pears
1   teaspoon grated lemon peel
      (set aside)
3   tablespoons lemon juice
1   cup sugar
2   tablespoons all-purpose flour
½ cup all-purpose flour
½ teaspoon ground ginger
½ teaspoon ground cinnamon
⅛ teaspoon ground mace
¼ cup butter *or* margarine

Prepare and roll out pastry into a 12-inch circle. Line a 9-inch pie plate. Trim to ½ inch beyond edge. Flute edge; do not prick pastry. Sprinkle pears with lemon juice. In a bowl combine ½ *cup* of the sugar, the 2 tablespoons flour, and lemon peel; stir in pears. Spoon pear-sugar mixture into pastry-lined plate. In another bowl combine the remaining ½ cup sugar, ½ cup flour, ginger, cinnamon, and mace. Cut in butter till mixture resembles coarse crumbs. Sprinkle crumb mixture over pear filling. To prevent overbrowning, cover edge of pie with foil. Bake in 375° oven for 25 minutes. Remove foil; bake for 25 to 30 minutes more or till pie is bubbly. Cool. If desired, garnish with cheese triangles.

Pineapples

Selecting: Since pineapples do not ripen after harvest, choose those that are at the peak of ripeness and flavor. Pineapples should be plump, slightly soft to the touch, fresh looking, and heavy for their size. The crown leaves should be deep green in color. The shell color, thumping, or the ease with which leaves can be pulled out are not reliable indications of ripeness or quality. Avoid pineapples that are old looking and that have dry, brown leaves, traces of mold, or an unpleasant odor. Fresh pineapples are available year-round, with peak supplies available from March through July.

Storing: The sooner a pineapple is used after purchase, the better it will be. Holding at room temperature causes softening and acid loss, but will not cause this fruit to ripen. An uncut pineapple may be refrigerated 1 to 2 days. After the crown and rind have been removed, the flesh of the pineapple may be kept a few days longer in the refrigerator.

Serving: Fresh pineapples may be eaten plain, used with cheese as an appetizer, pureed for use in beverages, or used in quick breads and salads, with meats and in desserts. Fresh pineapple for use with gelatin should always be cooked first; if used uncooked, the pineapple will prevent the gelatin from setting.

Gourmandise Cheese Ball

1   8-ounce can crushed
    pineapple (juice pack)
8   ounces gourmandise, softened
2   3-ounce packages cream
    cheese, softened
½   cup chopped pecans

Drain pineapple, reserving 2 tablespoons juice. In small mixer bowl beat softened gourmandise, cream cheese, and reserved pineapple juice till well blended. Stir in pineapple. Chill thoroughly. Shape into a ball; roll in pecans. Chill till serving time. Serve with crackers and fresh fruit slices. Makes about 2 cups.

Summer Ambrosia Salad

3   medium oranges
1   small fresh pineapple *or*
    one 15½-ounce can
    pineapple chunks,
    drained
½   cup drained maraschino
    cherries, halved
½   cup flaked *or* shredded
    coconut

Peel and section oranges over a bowl to catch juice. Combine orange sections and juice; set aside. Remove crown from pineapple. Peel pineapple; remove eyes and core. Cut pineapple into 1-inch chunks; measure 2 cups (save remainder for another use). Combine orange sections and juice, the pineapple chunks, and maraschino cherries. Cover and chill. Just before serving, fold in coconut. Makes 4 to 6 servings.

24-Hour Fruit Salad

2 cups fresh *or* frozen pitted dark sweet cherries
1 small fresh pineapple *or* one 20-ounce can pineapple chunks, drained
3 medium oranges
3 slightly beaten egg yolks
2 tablespoons sugar
2 tablespoons vinegar
1 tablespoon butter *or* margarine
2 cups tiny marshmallows
½ cup whipping cream

Thaw cherries, if frozen. Remove crown from pineapple; peel. Remove eyes and core. Cut pineapple into 1-inch chunks (should yield about 2½ cups). Peel and section oranges over a bowl to catch juice; reserve 2 tablespoons of the juice. For custard, in heavy saucepan combine reserved orange juice, egg yolks, sugar, vinegar, butter or margarine, and ⅛ teaspoon *salt*. Cook and stir over low heat about 6 minutes or till mixture thickens slightly. Chill about 10 minutes. Combine cherries, pineapple chunks, orange sections, and marshmallows. Pour cooled custard over; toss gently. Beat whipping cream just till soft peaks form; fold into fruit mixture. Turn into serving bowl. Cover and refrigerate 24 hours. Makes 10 to 12 servings.

Sweet-Sour Shrimp

12 ounces fresh *or* frozen shelled shrimp
1 8-ounce can pineapple chunks (juice pack)
1 medium green pepper, cut into strips
½ cup carrot bias sliced ¼ inch thick
1 clove garlic, minced
2 tablespoons cooking oil
1 cup chicken broth
½ cup packed brown sugar
⅓ cup vinegar
⅓ cup tomato sauce
2 teaspoons soy sauce
6 tablespoons cornstarch
1 beaten egg
¼ cup all-purpose flour
Cooking oil *or* shortening for deep fat frying

Thaw shrimp, if frozen. Drain pineapple chunks, reserving juice; set aside. In skillet cook green pepper, carrot, and garlic in 2 tablespoons oil till tender. Add reserved pineapple juice, ¾ cup of the chicken broth, brown sugar, vinegar, tomato sauce, and soy sauce to vegetable mixture. Bring to boiling. Blend 2 tablespoons of the cornstarch and 2 tablespoons *cold water*. Blend into vegetable mixture. Cook and stir till thickened and bubbly. Keep warm.

For batter, in small bowl combine egg, flour, remaining 4 tablespoons cornstarch, remaining chicken broth, and ½ teaspoon *salt*; beat till smooth. Dip shrimp in batter. Fry half at a time in deep, hot oil (365°) about 5 minutes or till golden. Drain; keep warm. Stir shrimp into sauce along with pineapple chunks. Heat through. If desired, serve over hot cooked rice. Makes 4 to 6 servings.

Pineapple Bread Pudding

¼ cup butter *or* margarine, softened
1 4-serving-size package *instant* vanilla pudding mix
1 teaspoon ground cinnamon
3 eggs
3 cups milk
1 8-ounce can crushed pineapple (juice pack)
⅔ cup flaked coconut
½ cup raisins
1 teaspoon vanilla
8 slices day-old white bread, cut into ½-inch cubes

In a large mixer bowl cream together butter or margarine, vanilla pudding mix, and cinnamon till fluffy. Add eggs, one at a time, beating well after each addition. In another bowl combine milk, *undrained* pineapple, coconut, raisins, and vanilla. By hand, blend milk mixture into creamed mixture (mixture will look curdled). Fold in bread cubes. Pour into an ungreased 2-quart casserole or 8x8x2-inch baking dish. Place casserole or baking dish in larger shallow pan on oven rack. Pour hot water into larger pan to a depth of 1 inch. Bake in 325° oven 1¼ hours for casserole (1 hour for baking dish) or till knife inserted near center comes out clean. Makes 8 servings.

Pineapple preserves give a bright glaze to this mixture of pineapple, orange slices, ham, sweet potatoes, and pea pods in *Ham Hawaiian*. A wok provides quick-cooking ease.

Ham Hawaiian

2 medium sweet potatoes *or* yams
1 small fresh pineapple *or* one 20-ounce can pineapple chunks, drained
½ teaspoon instant chicken bouillon granules
½ cup water
8 slices fully cooked ham (about 1 pound)
1 orange, halved and thinly sliced
1 6-ounce package frozen pea pods, thawed
½ cup pineapple preserves
2 tablespoons butter *or* margarine

In covered saucepan cook sweet potatoes or yams in enough boiling salted water to cover for 30 minutes or just till tender. Peel; halve lengthwise and crosswise. Remove crown from pineapple. Peel pineapple; remove eyes and core. Cut pineapple into 1-inch chunks (makes 2½ cups). In wok or large skillet dissolve bouillon granules in water. Place a heat-proof trivet or rack over liquid in pan.

Arrange sweet potatoes, pineapple chunks, ham slices, and orange slices on rack. Cover tightly with lid or foil. Bring to boil; reduce heat and simmer for 10 minutes or till heated through. Add thawed pea pods. Replace cover and steam for 2 to 3 minutes longer.

In saucepan combine pineapple preserves and butter or margarine. Cook and stir till heated through. Drizzle over ham mixture. Makes 4 servings.

Individual Pineapple Meringue Desserts

1 small fresh pineapple
1 cup fresh *or* frozen whole unsweetened strawberries, halved
¼ cup pineapple preserves
2 tablespoons peach *or* other fruit-flavored brandy
Dash ground ginger
2 egg whites
¼ teaspoon cream of tartar
¼ teaspoon vanilla
¼ cup packed brown sugar

Remove crown from pineapple. Peel pineapple; remove eyes and core. Cut pineapple into 1-inch chunks. In medium saucepan combine pineapple chunks and halved strawberries. In small bowl combine preserves, brandy, and ginger; stir into pineapple chunks and strawberries. Heat and stir just till warm. Spoon into four individual soufflé dishes.

In small mixer bowl beat egg whites with cream of tartar and vanilla at medium speed till soft peaks form. Gradually add brown sugar, beating till stiff peaks form. Spread meringue over entire surface of each pineapple mixture, sealing to edges. Place soufflé dishes in shallow baking pan. Bake in 350° oven for 12 minutes or till meringue is golden. Serve warm. Makes 4 servings.

Pineapple Upside-Down Cake

1 8¼-ounce can pineapple slices
2 tablespoons butter *or* margarine
½ cup packed brown sugar
4 maraschino cherries, halved
¾ cup granulated sugar
⅓ cup shortening
1 egg
1½ teaspoons vanilla
1½ cups all-purpose flour
2½ teaspoons baking powder
¼ teaspoon salt

Drain pineapple, reserving liquid. Halve pineapple slices crosswise. Melt butter or margarine in 9x1½-inch round baking pan. Stir in brown sugar and *1 tablespoon* of the reserved pineapple liquid. Add enough water to remaining pineapple liquid to measure ⅔ cup. Arrange pineapple and cherries in bottom of pan.

In small mixer bowl cream together granulated sugar and shortening till well combined. Add egg and vanilla; beat till fluffy. Stir together flour, baking powder, and salt; add to creamed mixture alternately with the ⅔ cup pineapple liquid, beating well after each addition. Carefully spread over pineapple layer in pan. Bake in 350° oven about 40 minutes or till cake tests done. Cool on wire rack for 5 minutes; invert onto serving plate; serve warm.

Plums

Selecting: *Look for plums that have good color for their variety, yield to gentle pressure, and that are slightly soft at the tip end. There are more than 2,000 varieties of plums. The two main types are the Japanese and the European. The Japanese plums, medium to large in size with red or yellow skin color, are very juicy and are found in a variety of shapes. The European varieties are smaller, milder in flavor, and firmer in texture than the Japanese. They are oval or round in shape and are blue or purple in color. Prunes are actually a type of European plum that can be dried without fermenting. All prune plums are freestone (the pits separate readily from the flesh). Standard plums are clingstones. Italian prune plums are the best known type of plum used for drying. The varieties shown here are, from back left: Italian Prune Plum, Friar, Casselman, Kelsey, and Elephant Heart. Plums are available from June through September, with peak supplies available in July and August.*

Storing: *Ripen plums at room temperature. Refrigerate uncovered, and use within 3 to 5 days.*

Serving: *Most popular as a snack or in desserts, plums also are excellent in blender drinks, salads, coffee cakes, sauces, and as a meat accompaniment.*

Spicy Plum Salad

6 fresh plums, pitted and chopped *or* one 8½-ounce can whole, unpitted purple plums, drained, pitted, and chopped
⅓ cup dry white wine
1 6-ounce package raspberry-flavored gelatin
½ teaspoon ground cinnamon
⅛ teaspoon ground cloves
2 fresh plums (optional)
　Dairy sour cream

Combine chopped plums and wine; let stand for 3 hours at room temperature. In large bowl combine gelatin, cinnamon, and cloves; add 2 cups *boiling water*, stirring till gelatin is dissolved. Drain chopped plums, reserving wine. Stir reserved wine and 1 cup *cold water* into gelatin mixture. Chill gelatin mixture till partially set (consistency of unbeaten egg whites); stir in chopped plums. Pour into a 6½-cup fluted ring mold. If desired, slice and pit the 2 fresh plums; arrange in the mold before carefully pouring in the gelatin mixture. Chill till firm. If desired, unmold onto lettuce-lined plate. Serve topped with sour cream. Serves 8 to 10.

Spicy Plum Salad is studded with juicy plums and accented with
cinnamon and cloves; white wine adds a delicate flavor to complement the fruit.

Plum-Sauced Lamb Chops

12 fresh plums *or* one 16-ounce can whole, unpitted purple plums, drained
¼ cup dry white wine
1 tablespoon lemon juice
1 tablespoon soy sauce
½ teaspoon worcestershire sauce
¼ teaspoon dried basil, crushed
⅛ teaspoon garlic powder
8 lamb rib chops, cut 1 inch thick
4 nectarines *or* peaches, peeled, pitted, and halved

Pit plums. For marinade, in blender container combine plums, wine, lemon juice, soy sauce, worcestershire, basil, and garlic powder. Cover and blend till smooth. Place lamb in a plastic bag. Set in a pan. Pour marinade over lamb. Close bag; turn to evenly distribute marinade. Cover and let stand overnight in refrigerator; turn occasionally. Drain; reserve marinade.

Place chops on unheated rack of broiler pan. Broil 3 to 4 inches from heat for 6 minutes. Turn chops. Add nectarine or peach halves to broiler pan; brush with marinade. Broil 6 to 7 minutes longer or till lamb is done. Heat remaining marinade; pass with meat and fruit. If desired, garnish with watercress. Makes 4 servings.

Plum-Filled Ladder Loaf (pictured on page 4)

½ cup milk
¼ cup butter *or* margarine
3 tablespoons granulated sugar
1 13¾-ounce package hot roll mix
2 beaten eggs
6 fresh plums, pitted and chopped *or* one 8½-ounce can whole, unpitted purple plums, drained, pitted, and chopped
1 cup packed brown sugar
½ cup finely chopped toasted almonds
½ cup fine dry bread crumbs
½ teaspoon ground cinnamon
Confectioners' Icing (see recipe, page 21)
Toasted sliced almonds

In small saucepan heat milk, butter or margarine, and granulated sugar just till warm (110° to 115°) and butter or margarine is almost melted; stir constantly. Remove from heat. Add yeast from hot roll mix; stir to dissolve. In mixing bowl combine flour from hot roll mix, warm milk mixture, and eggs; stir till well-combined. Turn out onto well-floured surface and knead till smooth (about 5 minutes). Place in lightly greased bowl; turn once to grease surface. Cover and let rise in a warm place till double (about 1 hour).

Punch down; divide in half. Cover and let rest 10 minutes. Combine plums, brown sugar, ½ cup finely chopped almonds, bread crumbs, and cinnamon. Roll half of the dough to a 9-inch square. Place on greased baking sheet. Spread half of the plum mixture down center of dough. With kitchen shears snip sides toward center in strips 3 inches long and 1 inch wide. Fold strips over filling, alternating from side to side. Repeat with remaining dough and plum mixture. Cover; let rise till nearly double (about 40 minutes). Bake in 350° oven for 25 minutes or till golden brown. Cover loosely with foil the last 15 minutes of baking to prevent overbrowning. Cool; drizzle with Confectioners' Icing and sprinkle with additional toasted almonds. Makes 2 coffee cakes.

Plum-Good Parfaits

12 fresh plums *or* one 30-ounce can whole, unpitted purple plums, drained
⅔ cup sugar
1 tablespoon cornstarch
Dash ground cinnamon
Dash ground cloves
1 tablespoon lemon juice
Vanilla ice cream

Pit and slice plums. In medium saucepan combine sugar, cornstarch, cinnamon, cloves, and dash *salt*. Stir in plums and lemon juice. Bring to boiling. Reduce heat and simmer, covered, for 8 to 10 minutes; cool. Layer with vanilla ice cream in parfait glasses. Makes 6 servings.

Rhubarb

Selecting: *Rhubarb, a member of the buckwheat family, is a vegetable, but because of its use it is often thought of as a fruit. Fresh rhubarb stalks should be firm, crisp, tender, and either cherry red or pink in color. The younger stalks usually have the most tender and delicate flavor. Choose stalks that are fairly thick but avoid those that are extremely thick or very thin, because they may be rough, fibrous, and stringy. Avoid rhubarb that isn't fresh and has a wilted, flabby appearance. Rhubarb, grown year-round in the field or in hothouses, is in peak supply from January through June.*

Storing: *Rhubarb wilts rapidly at room temperature and must be kept cool. Store stalks in the crisper section of the refrigerator and use within a few days.*

Serving: *Only the stalk of the rhubarb is edible because the leaves contain oxalic acid. If eaten in quantity they could be fatal. The flavor of raw rhubarb is strongly acidic, but is pleasingly tart when cooked and sweetened. Because of its familiar use in pies, rhubarb is frequently referred to as "pieplant." Rhubarb is also popular for use in beverages, sauces, salads, puddings, jams and jellies, tarts, coffee cakes, pies, and other baked desserts.*

Rhubarb Crush

- 1 **pound fresh rhubarb, cut into ½-inch pieces (3 cups)**
- ¾ **cup sugar**
- 1 **6-ounce can frozen pink lemonade concentrate**
  Crushed ice
- 1 **16-ounce bottle lemon-lime carbonated beverage, chilled**

In saucepan combine rhubarb, sugar, lemonade concentrate, and 3 cups *water*. Bring to boiling; reduce heat. Cover and simmer for 10 minutes or till rhubarb is very tender. Strain to remove pulp; chill the syrup. Just before serving, pour rhubarb syrup over crushed ice in tall glasses, filling glasses about ⅔ full. Carefully pour carbonated beverage in each glass. If desired, garnish with lemon slices. Makes 6 (8-ounce) servings.

Rhubarb Sauce

- ½ to ⅔ **cup sugar**
- ¼ **cup water**
- 1 **orange peel strip (optional)**
- 1 **pound fresh rhubarb, cut into ½-inch pieces (3 cups)** *or* **one 16-ounce package frozen rhubarb, thawed**

Combine sugar, water, and orange peel. Bring to boiling; add rhubarb. Reduce heat. Cover and simmer 5 minutes or till rhubarb is tender. Remove orange peel. If desired, serve over cake or ice cream. Makes 2 cups.

Strawberry-Rhubarb Sauce: Prepare as directed above, except omit the orange peel and use ⅔ cup *sugar* and ⅓ cup *water*; add ¼ teaspoon finely shredded *lemon peel* and 2 tablespoons *lemon juice*. After rhubarb is cooked, add 1 cup fresh or frozen unsweetened *strawberries*, sliced, and ¼ teaspoon ground *cinnamon*. Heat through. If desired, stir in 2 tablespoons *brandy*. Makes 3 cups.

Rhubarb-Strawberry Coffee Cake

3 cups all-purpose flour
1 cup sugar
1 teaspoon baking soda
1 teaspoon baking powder
1 teaspoon salt
1 cup butter *or* margarine
1 cup buttermilk
2 slightly beaten eggs
1 teaspoon vanilla
  Rhubarb Filling
¾ cup sugar
½ cup all-purpose flour
¼ cup butter *or* margarine

Stir together 3 cups flour, 1 cup sugar, soda, baking powder, and salt. Cut in 1 cup butter to fine crumbs. Beat together buttermilk, eggs, and vanilla; add to dry ingredients. Stir to moisten. Spread *half* the batter in greased 13x9x2-inch baking pan. Spread cooled filling over batter in pan. Spoon remaining batter in small mounds atop filling. Combine remaining sugar and flour; cut in ¼ cup butter to fine crumbs. Sprinkle crumbs over batter in pan. Bake in 350° oven for 40 to 45 minutes. Makes 12 to 15 servings.

Rhubarb Filling: In saucepan combine 1 pound fresh rhubarb, cut into 1-inch pieces (3 cups) *or* one 16-ounce package frozen *rhubarb*, and one 16-ounce package frozen sliced *strawberries*, thawed. Cover and cook about 5 minutes. Add 2 tablespoons *lemon juice*. Combine 1 cup *sugar* and ⅓ cup *cornstarch*; add to rhubarb mixture. Cook and stir till thickened and bubbly; cool.

Fresh Rhubarb Betty

2 medium oranges
1½ cups sugar
1 tablespoon all-purpose flour
¼ teaspoon salt
1½ pounds fresh rhubarb, cut into ½-inch pieces (4½ cups)
4 cups soft bread crumbs (about 5½ slices)
½ cup butter *or* margarine, melted
½ cup flaked coconut

Finely shred 1 teaspoon orange peel. Peel, section, and dice oranges (about ⅔ cup); set aside. In large bowl combine sugar, flour, salt, and ½ *teaspoon* of the shredded orange peel. Stir in rhubarb and diced oranges. Add 2 *cups* of the bread crumbs and ¼ *cup* of the melted butter; toss lightly. Turn into 12x7½x2-inch baking dish. Combine remaining bread crumbs, remaining ¼ cup melted butter, remaining orange peel, and the coconut. Sprinkle over the rhubarb mixture. Bake in 350° oven about 40 minutes or till golden. Serve warm. Makes 6 to 8 servings.

Rhubarb Custard Pie

Pastry for a Single-Crust Pie
  (see recipe, page 22)
1 cup sugar
3 tablespoons all-purpose flour
¼ teaspoon salt
3 egg yolks
3 tablespoons frozen orange juice concentrate
2 tablespoons butter *or* margarine, softened
1 pound fresh rhubarb, cut into ½-inch pieces (3 cups) *or* one 16-ounce package frozen rhubarb, thawed
3 egg whites
⅓ cup sugar
⅓ cup chopped pecans

Prepare and roll pastry into a 12-inch circle. Line a 9-inch pie plate. Trim pastry to ½ inch beyond edge of pie plate. Flute edge; do not prick pastry.

In large bowl combine 1 cup sugar, flour, and salt. Add egg yolks, juice concentrate, and butter or margarine; beat till smooth with rotary beater. Stir in rhubarb. Beat egg whites till soft peaks form (tips curl over). Gradually add ⅓ cup sugar, beating till stiff peaks form (tips stand straight). Gently fold whites into rhubarb mixture. Pour into pastry shell; sprinkle with nuts. Bake in 325° oven for 55 minutes. If desired, garnish with whipped cream.

The complementary flavors of rhubarb and strawberries
team up in the moist filling of *Rhubarb-Strawberry Coffee Cake*.

Exotic Fruits

Selecting: Shown here, clockwise from top, are: coconuts, plantains, papayas, quinces, figs, kiwis, litchis, guavas, and mangoes. Coconuts should contain milk and be heavy for their size. Plantains appear similar to green bananas, but are not as sweet and are longer and thicker than bananas. The skins are rough and blemished. Papayas are pear-shaped, melon-like fruits. Choose those with smooth, unblemished skin. Allow firm papayas to ripen at room temperature for three to five days or until the fruit yields to gentle pressure. Papayas, coconuts, and plantains, are available throughout the year. Quince, an autumn fruit, resembles an apple with a misshapen stem end. Look for quinces that are firm, smooth, blemish-free, and pale yellow when fully ripe. Figs vary according to variety in shape and color of their skin and flesh. When ripe, they are fairly soft to the touch. Figs are highly perishable and will sour and ferment when overripe. Kiwi fruits are lemon-shaped, with a soft, brown, fuzzy skin. Choose firm kiwis and allow to ripen at room temperature for two to three days. Figs are available in the summer and early fall. Kiwis are on the market from June to March. Litchis (or lichees), available in early summer, are eaten dried (litchi nuts) or fresh. Only the pulp, which has a flavor similar to Royal Anne cherries, is edible. Guavas vary in size, shape, color, and flavor. The fruit has small seeds embedded in the flesh and a skin color of green to yellow. Most guavas are processed, so this fruit is seldom on the market. Choose mangoes that are smooth and firm. Allow them to ripen at room temperature until softened. Mangoes are at peak availability during the summer.

Storing: Coconuts may be refrigerated one to two months. Quinces will keep for a long time when stored in a cool, dry place. Kiwis and litchis will keep for several weeks in the refrigerator. Plantains should not be refrigerated unless they become soft. Papayas and mangoes will keep for a few days in the refrigerator. Figs and guavas should be used as soon as possible, but refrigerate if held briefly.

Serving: Quinces and guavas are popular for use in jam and jelly-making. Plantains are always eaten cooked, and may be fried and served as a meat accompaniment. Serve fresh kiwis, litchis, papayas, mangoes, or figs to add an unusual touch to salads and desserts. Other exotic fruits to enjoy are: pomegranates, persimmons, ugli fruits, granadillas (passion fruit), carambolas, prickly pears, papaws, and cherimoyas.

Green and Gold Salad

⅓ cup salad oil
3 tablespoons vinegar
1 tablespoon sugar
2 teaspoons lemon *or* lime juice
¼ teaspoon paprika
2 large fresh papayas
6 cups mixed salad greens
1 medium cucumber, sliced

In shaker jar combine oil, vinegar, sugar, lemon or lime juice, paprika, and ¼ teaspoon *salt*. Cover and shake till blended. Chill. Peel, seed, and slice papayas lengthwise. In large salad bowl combine greens, papaya, and cucumber. Cover and chill. At serving time, shake dressing and pour over salad. Toss lightly. Makes 6 to 8 servings.

Quince Curried Ham Loaf

2 beaten eggs
½ cup milk
1½ cups soft bread crumbs
    (2 slices)
⅓ cup finely chopped onion
1½ pounds ground fully cooked
    ham
1 pound ground pork
2 quinces, peeled and cored
2 apples, peeled and cored
¼ cup packed brown sugar
1 to 1½ teaspoons curry powder

In large bowl combine eggs and milk; stir in crumbs and onion. Add meats and mix well. Shape into an oval 8x6-inch loaf in 12x7½x2-inch baking dish. Bake in 350° oven for 1 hour. Spoon off excess fat. Cut quinces and apples into wedges; arrange around ham loaf. In small bowl combine brown sugar and curry; stir in ½ cup *water*. Drizzle over fruits. Return to oven. Bake 15 minutes more. Turn fruits; continue baking 15 minutes more. Makes 8 servings.

Mango Mousse

2 15-ounce jars mango slices
2 envelopes unflavored gelatin
½ cup sugar
½ cup water
1 tablespoon lemon juice
4 egg whites
1 cup whipping cream
1 tablespoon lemon juice

Drain *one* jar mangoes, reserving syrup; refrigerate mangoes. Place second jar undrained mangoes in blender container. Cover and blend till nearly smooth; strain to remove seeds. Set aside. Combine gelatin and sugar; add the water. Heat and stir till sugar and gelatin are dissolved. Add strained mangoes, reserved syrup, and 1 tablespoon lemon juice; gradually stir into unbeaten egg whites. Chill till partially set. Whip till light. Whip cream till soft peaks form; fold into gelatin. Turn mixture into 6-cup mold; chill till firm. To prepare sauce, in blender container blend chilled mangoes till smooth; strain. Stir in remaining lemon juice. Unmold mousse onto serving plate and serve with sauce. Serves 8.

Ugli Fruit in Spiced Wine

4 ugli fruit
½ cup dry red wine
¼ cup sugar
2 tablespoons lemon juice
  Dash ground cinnamon
  Dash ground cloves

Remove peel and outer membrane from fruit. Using a bowl to catch juices and starting near center of fruit, insert blade of a table knife between a section of fruit and the dividing membrane. Slide blade toward the outside. Repeat along other side of section. Place fruit in bowl with juices. In saucepan mix wine, sugar, lemon juice, and spices. Heat till sugar dissolves. Pour hot liquid over fruit and juices. Serve warm or chilled. Makes 6 servings.

Discover the taste of the tropics with *Exotic Fruit Platter*. Present these lush fruits on ti (pronounced "tea") leaves, available at most florist shops.

Exotic Fruit Platter

1 3-ounce package cream
   cheese, softened
⅓ cup pineapple preserves
1 tablespoon milk
½ teaspoon finely shredded
   lemon peel
2 teaspoons lemon juice
½ cup whipping cream
   Ti leaves *or* lettuce
3 fresh medium mangoes,
   peeled, seeded, and sliced
2 kiwi fruits, peeled and sliced
⅓ cup pomegranate seeds
   (optional)

For dressing, blend cream cheese and preserves. Stir in milk, lemon peel, and lemon juice. Whip cream just till soft peaks form; fold into cream cheese mixture. Cover and chill. Line a platter with ti leaves or lettuce. Arrange mango and kiwi fruit slices atop. If desired, sprinkle with pomegranate seeds. Serve fruit with dressing. If desired, garnish dressing with lemon peel twist. Makes 6 servings.

Persimmon Pudding

1 cup all-purpose flour
1 cup granulated sugar
1 teaspoon baking soda
¼ teaspoon salt
1 cup mashed persimmons
   (about 5 persimmons)
½ cup milk
1 tablespoon shortening, melted
1½ cups sifted powdered sugar
½ cup butter *or* margarine,
   softened
2 teaspoons vanilla

In large bowl combine flour, granulated sugar, baking soda, and salt. Combine persimmons, milk, and shortening. Stir into flour mixture. Pour batter into greased 9-inch quiche dish or pie plate. Place quiche dish or pie plate in large shallow pan. Set shallow pan on oven rack. Pour boiling water into pan to a depth of ½ inch. Bake in 350° oven for 1 to 1¼ hours, adding more water, if necessary. Remove quiche dish or pie plate to wire rack; cool slightly to serve warm or cool completely and chill to serve cold.

   Meanwhile, in small mixer bowl beat powdered sugar and butter or margarine till fluffy. Beat in vanilla. Serve over pudding. Makes 6 to 8 servings.

Coconut Cream Pie

  Pastry for Single-Crust Pie
    (see recipe, page 22)
1 cup sugar
½ cup all-purpose flour *or* ¼ cup
   cornstarch
¼ teaspoon salt
3 cups milk
4 slightly beaten egg yolks
1 3½-ounce can (1⅓ cups) flaked
   coconut
3 tablespoons butter *or*
   margarine
1½ teaspoons vanilla
4 egg whites
1 teaspoon vanilla
½ teaspoon cream of tartar
½ cup sugar

Prepare and roll out pastry into 12-inch circle. Transfer to 9-inch pie plate. Trim pastry to ½ inch beyond edge. Flute; prick pastry. Bake in 450° oven for 10 to 12 minutes. Cool. For filling, in saucepan combine 1 cup sugar, the flour or cornstarch, and salt. Stir in milk. Cook and stir till thickened and bubbly. Cook and stir 2 minutes more. Remove from heat. Gradually stir *1 cup* of the hot mixture into slightly beaten egg yolks. Return yolk mixture to saucepan; return to gentle boil. Cook and stir 2 minutes longer. Remove from heat. Stir in *1 cup* of the coconut, butter or margarine, and 1½ teaspoons vanilla. Pour hot filling into baked pastry shell.

   For meringue, in large mixer bowl beat egg whites, 1 teaspoon vanilla, and cream of tartar till soft peaks form. Gradually add ½ cup sugar, beating till stiff peaks form. Spread over hot filling; seal to edge. Sprinkle with remaining coconut. Bake in 350° oven for 12 to 15 minutes or till golden. Cool. Cover; chill to store.

   Banana Cream Pie: Prepare as directed above *except* omit coconut. Slice 3 *bananas* into bottom of pastry shell. Pour hot filling over bananas; top with meringue.

Dried Fruits

Selecting: Look for firm, meaty dried fruits that are free from dirt, mold, insects, and musty odor. Pictured clockwise from the top are: pears, Calimyrna figs, Black Mission figs, light raisins, apricots, currants, prunes, peaches, apples, and dark raisins. These fruits may be sun- or mechanically dried and are very often treated with sulfur dioxide to prevent darkening. Most dried fruits are packed in cartons or bags and are plentiful year-round.

Storing: The concentrated sugars in dried fruits serve as natural preservatives, so storage of dried fruits is relatively simple. Unopened packages of most dried fruits will keep for six to eight months when stored in a cool, dry place or in the refrigerator. During hot weather, however, dried fruits always should be stored in the refrigerator. Partially used packages of dried fruits should always be stored tightly covered.

Serving: Snack on dried fruits right from the package or cook up a batch using the directions, opposite. Raisins require no cooking, but may be plumped for added juiciness. To plump light or dark raisins, place in a saucepan and cover with water about 1 inch above raisins. Bring to boiling; remove from heat. Cover and let stand about 5 minutes; drain. Use raisins and other dried fruits in all kinds of breads, cakes, cookies, sauces, and compotes.

Harvest Fruit Mold

1   **11-ounce package mixed dried fruits**
1   **6-ounce package orange-flavored gelatin**
2   **cups boiling water**
½   **cup dry sherry**
     Lettuce

In saucepan combine dried fruits and enough water to cover the fruits. Bring to boiling; reduce heat. Cover and simmer for 20 to 25 minutes or till tender. Drain fruits, reserving liquid. Add enough water to the reserved liquid to measure 1½ cups. Dissolve gelatin in the 2 cups boiling water. Stir in the 1½ cups liquid and sherry. Chill till partially set (consistency of unbeaten egg whites).

Meanwhile, pit prunes; cut up cooked fruits. Fold fruits into partially set gelatin mixture. Turn into 6-cup mold. Chill for several hours or overnight or till firm. Unmold onto lettuce-lined plate. Makes 8 to 10 servings.

Apricot-Almond Coffee Cake

1 cup water
¾ cup dried apricots, finely snipped
  Milk
1½ cups all-purpose flour
¾ cup granulated sugar
2 teaspoons baking powder
½ teaspoon salt
½ teaspoon ground cinnamon
1 beaten egg
¼ cup cooking oil
¼ cup all-purpose flour
¼ cup packed brown sugar
2 tablespoons butter *or* margarine
¼ cup chopped almonds

In saucepan combine water and snipped apricots. Bring to boiling; reduce heat. Cover and simmer for 15 minutes. Cool. Drain, reserving liquid. Add enough milk to reserved liquid to measure ½ cup liquid.

In large bowl stir together 1½ cups flour, granulated sugar, baking powder, salt, and cinnamon. Combine egg, oil, and the reserved ½ cup liquid. Stir into the flour mixture. Stir in drained apricots. Turn into greased 9x9x2-inch baking pan.

In small bowl combine ¼ cup flour and brown sugar. Cut in butter or margarine till crumbly; stir in almonds. Sprinkle over batter. Bake in 350° oven for 40 to 45 minutes or till cake tests done. Makes 1 coffee cake.

Fruited Pot Roast

1 3-pound beef chuck pot roast
2 tablespoons shortening
1½ teaspoons salt
¼ teaspoon pepper
½ cup finely chopped onion
½ cup burgundy
⅓ cup finely chopped carrot
1 clove garlic, minced
1 11-ounce package mixed dried fruits
1½ cups hot water
⅓ cup cold water
3 tablespoons all-purpose flour

Trim excess fat from meat. In Dutch oven brown meat on all sides in hot shortening. Sprinkle with 1½ teaspoons salt and ¼ teaspoon pepper; add onion, burgundy, carrot, and garlic. Cover and simmer for 1½ hours.

Meanwhile, cut up large pieces of dried fruits. Pour 1½ cups hot water over fruits; let stand 1 hour. Drain fruits, reserving liquid. Place fruits over meat. Cover and cook about 45 minutes longer or till meat is tender.

Remove meat and drained fruits to serving platter and keep warm. For gravy, pour pan juices into measuring cup; skim off fat. Add reserved fruit liquid to pan juices in measuring cup to measure 1½ cups liquid; return to Dutch oven. Combine ⅓ cup cold water and flour; stir into liquid in Dutch oven. Cook and stir till mixture thickens and bubbles. Season to taste. Serve gravy with roast. Makes 6 to 8 servings.

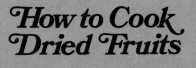

How to Cook Dried Fruits

Rinse fruits and cover with water 1 inch above fruits. Bring to boiling. Cover; simmer for time specified at right. (Some dried fruits are processed to cut cooking time; refer to package directions). If desired, add sugar during last 5 minutes of cooking.

DRIED FRUITS	COOKING TIME IN MINUTES	SUGAR PER CUP UNCOOKED FRUITS
apples	20 to 30	3 to 4 tablespoons
apricots	15 to 20	3 to 4 tablespoons
figs	35 to 40	1 tablespoon
mixed fruits	20 to 25	2 to 3 tablespoons
peaches	25 to 30	3 to 4 tablespoons
pears	20 to 25	3 to 4 tablespoons
prunes	10 to 15	2 tablespoons

Swedish Fruit Soup

1 **11-ounce package mixed dried fruits**
½ **cup light raisins**
3 **to 4 inches stick cinnamon**
2¼ **cups unsweetened pineapple juice**
2 **tablespoons quick-cooking tapioca**
1 **medium orange, thinly sliced and halved**
½ **cup currant jelly**
¼ **cup sugar**

In large saucepan combine mixed fruits, raisins, cinnamon, and 4 cups *water*. Bring to boiling; reduce heat. Simmer about 20 to 25 minutes or till fruits are tender.

Meanwhile combine pineapple juice and tapioca; let stand for 15 minutes. Add pineapple juice mixture, orange slices, jelly, sugar, and ¼ teaspoon *salt* to cooked fruits. Bring to boiling; reduce heat. Cover and simmer for 15 minutes longer, stirring occasionally. Remove stick cinnamon. Serve warm or cold. Makes 10 servings.

Hot Fruit Compote

2½ **cups pitted, dried prunes**
1⅓ **cups dried apricots**
1 **15½-ounce can pineapple chunks**
1 **21-ounce can cherry pie filling**
2 **cups water**
¼ **cup dry white wine**

In 9x9x2-inch baking pan layer prunes, apricots, and *undrained* pineapple. Combine cherry pie filling, water, and dry white wine. Pour over fruit. Cover and bake in 350° oven for 1½ hours or till dried fruits are tender. Serve warm. Makes 8 servings.

Currant Pound Cake

1 **cup dried currants**
¼ **cup brandy**
8 **eggs**
2¼ **cups sugar**
2 **cups butter *or* margarine, softened**
4 **cups all-purpose flour**
½ **teaspoon ground nutmeg**

In small bowl combine currants and brandy. Cover tightly and let stand at room temperature for several hours or overnight. Allow eggs to come to room temperature. Grease bottoms of two 9x5x3-inch loaf pans. In large mixer bowl cream sugar and butter or margarine till light. Add eggs, one at a time, beating well after each addition (about 10 minutes total beating time for eggs). Stir together flour and nutmeg; stir into creamed mixture. Drain currants well; fold into batter. Turn into prepared pans. Bake in 325° oven for 60 to 65 minutes or till cakes test done. Makes 2 cakes.

Lemon-Raisin Pie

Pastry for Single-Crust Pie (see recipe, page 22)
1½ **cups raisins**
6 **slightly beaten eggs**
1½ **cups sugar**
½ **cup coarsely chopped walnuts**
¼ **cup lemon juice**
¼ **cup butter *or* margarine, melted**
½ **teaspoon ground cinnamon**
½ **teaspoon ground nutmeg**
¼ **teaspoon salt**

Prepare and roll out pastry into a 12-inch circle. Transfer to 9-inch pie plate. Trim to ½ inch beyond edge. Flute edge high. Bake in 450° oven for 5 minutes. Cool.

To plump raisins, place in medium saucepan. Cover with water 1 inch above raisins. Bring to boiling; remove from heat. Cover and let stand for 5 minutes; drain.

For filling, in large bowl combine eggs, sugar, nuts, lemon juice, butter or margarine, cinnamon, nutmeg, salt, and plumped raisins; mix well. Place pie shell on oven rack; pour filling into shell. To prevent overbrowning, cover edge of pie with foil. Bake in 375° oven for 20 minutes. Remove foil. Bake for 20 minutes longer or till knife inserted off-center comes out clean. Cool. Cover; chill.

Swedish Fruit Soup blends the sweet, mellow flavors of dried fruits with
the tart taste of orange and pineapple. Serve this soup warm or chilled for dessert.

3 FRUIT PRESERVING PRIMER

Whether you grow fruits in your garden or buy them at the grocer's stand, you can learn how to preserve their flavors, colors, and textures. This primer explains canning, freezing, and making jelly.

Fruit Juice Jelly
(page 91)
Frozen Melons
(page 87)
Spiced Peaches
(page 88)
Apple-Grapefruit Marmalade (page 93)
Cherry-Raspberry Jam
(page 92)

CANNING BASICS

Canning is an effective way to preserve fresh fruits for good eating every day of the year. By following a few basic canning rules you can prevent bacteria, yeasts, and molds normally present in the soil, air, and on kitchen work surfaces from causing food spoilage or illness. The proper combination of temperature and time is necessary to destroy harmful organisms in fresh fruits and is essential for successful canning. These easy-to-follow canning basics help assure safe, satisfying results.

Assembling the equipment: Useful canning equipment is illustrated at right. Included is a boiling water bath canner which is a large, deep kettle fitted with a rack or basket for jars and a tight-fitting lid. You may buy a boiling water bath canner or improvise with a big kettle you already own. A boiling water bath canner should be deep enough to allow 1 to 2 inches of water to boil vigorously over the tops of jars during processing. The rack or basket separates the jars and keeps them off the bottom, ensuring proper heat penetration. The lid prevents steam from billowing out.

Glass canning jars, also known as mason jars, are the standard containers used in home canning. These reusable jars are produced in a variety of sizes ranging from ½ pint to ½ gallon. The glass is tempered to withstand heat. In addition, the jars have threaded mouths so popular flat metal lids with screw bands or the less common zinc caps with rubber rings make airtight seals.

Flat metal lids with metal screw bands are the most common type of caps for home-canned products. Flat metal lids are designed for one-time usage, but screw bands may be reused as long as they are not bent out of shape. Zinc caps with porcelain linings and rubber rings were the first caps developed for use with mason jars. Although zinc caps and rubber rings are still produced, their popularity is declining.

Preparing the syrup: Select a syrup to suit the sweetness of the fruits to be canned—and the sweetness level you prefer. Measure the desired amount of sugar and water into a saucepan. Bring to boiling; keep warm. For Very Light Syrup, use 1 cup sugar with 4 cups water to yield 4½ cups syrup. For Light Syrup, use 2 cups sugar with 4 cups water to yield 5 cups syrup. For Medium Syrup, use 3 cups sugar with 4 cups water to yield 5½ cups syrup. For Heavy Syrup, use 4¾ cups sugar with 4 cups water to yield 6½ cups syrup. (Editors Note: We prefer the sweetness of Very Light Syrup for most fruits, even though fruits canned in light syrups are sometimes less firm than fruits canned in heavy syrups.)

Getting fruits ready: The goodness of canned fruits depends on their initial quality. The higher the quality and the shorter the time between garden and canner, the better the final canned product. Choose only fresh, firm-yet-ripe fruits. Sort according to size, color, and maturity. Wash fruits thoroughly but gently. Work quickly to do the necessary peeling, coring, or cutting so fruits go into jars without long periods of soaking or standing. Prepare enough fruit to fill 1 canner at a time.

Filling the jars: Examine jars for flaws around rims. Discard jars with chips or cracks. Wash jars in sudsy water; rinse. Pour hot water over and let stand till ready to fill; drain.

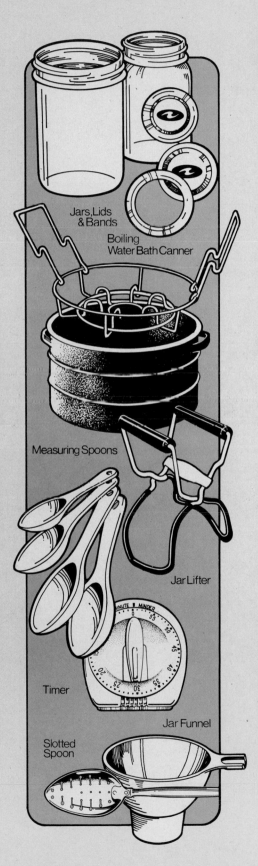

Jars, Lids & Bands
Boiling Water Bath Canner
Measuring Spoons
Jar Lifter
Timer
Jar Funnel
Slotted Spoon

CANNING BASICS *continued*

Spoon fruit (peaches) into hot, clean jars. Leave ½ inch headspace between top of fruit and rim of jar.

Place jars in canner; add boiling water to bring water level 1 or 2 inches above the tops of jars.

Test for proper sealing by looking for a dip in the center of lid and then feeling for it with your finger.

To fill jars, set on a cloth. Fill jars using either the cold (raw) pack or hot pack method. You'll find both methods in the Canning and Freezing Guide (pages 84 to 89) unless a particular fruit is best when canned only one way.

For cold (raw) pack, fill jars with uncooked fruit, leaving ½ inch headspace. Headspace is the distance between the top of the fruit and the rim of the jar and is important for proper sealing. For hot pack, precook fruit, then pack the hot fruit loosely into canning jars, leaving ½ inch headspace.

Use a ladle to add enough boiling syrup or water to cold- or hot-packed fruit to cover, again leaving ½ inch headspace. Chase out air bubbles with a flexible spatula; add more boiling syrup or water to jars, if necessary, to maintain proper headspace. Wipe jar rims and threads. Place flat metal lid with sealing compound next to glass; screw the metal band down firmly.

For both cold- and hot-pack, fill 1 jar at a time with fruit and then syrup. Immediately cover with lid and band as directed above.

Processing the jars: Set the boiling water bath canner containing a rack on the kitchen range. Fill with 4 or 5 inches of water. Cover and heat. At the same time, begin heating additional water which eventually will be used to fill the canner after all the jars are in place. (Since this initial heating may take some time, it is a good idea to start heating water early, even before you begin syrup or fruit preparation.) When the water in the canner is hot, fill jars as directed above and place on rack in the canner. Replace cover each time you add a jar so the minimum of steam escapes. When the last jar is added to the canner, check the water level. Using additional boiling water, fill the canner so water is 1 to 2 inches above the tops of jars. Cover and continue heating until water comes to a full rolling boil. Now start counting the processing time. Times for various jar sizes are given in each recipe in the Canning and Freezing Guide (pages 84 to 89). Times listed are for fruits canned at sea level. (Add 1 minute processing for each 1,000 feet above sea level when processing time specified is 20 minutes or less. Add 2 minutes for each 1,000 feet above sea level when processing time is more than 20 minutes.) Adjust heat under canner so water boils gently during entire processing time. When processing is completed, turn off heat. Use a jar lifter to transfer hot jars to a cloth or board.

Testing the seals: The canning job is not done until jars are sealed. You may hear a loud snap while the jars are cooling, but sealing is not always accompanied by a noise. When jars are completely cooled, flat metal lids are sealed if centers are dipped and stay down when pressed. Unsealed jars must be repacked and processed with a new lid. If only one jar didn't seal, refrigerate it and use within a day or two.

Storing the jars: Label jars, listing contents and date, and store in a dark, cool, dry place. Home-canned products lose quality rapidly if stored in a warm room.

Detecting Spoilage: Leakage from jars, patches of mold, and a foamy or murky appearance are signs that the product has spoiled. If it doesn't look or smell right, don't eat it.

FREEZING BASICS

Freezing captures the fresh flavor and bright natural color of fruits for year-round enjoyment. Freezing preserves the fruits by retarding the growth of bacteria, yeasts, and molds and slowing other chemical changes.

Assembling the equipment: Except for packaging materials, home freezing requires only the equipment found in most kitchens (see illustration at right).

Packaging materials for frozen fruits should be moistureproof and vaporproof to prevent loss of moisture or contact with air. Rigid plastic freezer containers, available in pint, 1½ pint, quart, and 2 quart sizes, are common. Freezing jars with wide mouths and tapered sides also are popular, available in ½ pint, pint, and 1½ pint sizes. Both rigid plastic containers and glass jars are excellent for freezing fruits packed in syrup, sugar, or water. Plastic freezer bags, available in a multitude of sizes, are handy for freezing fruits when no syrup, sugar, or water is added.

Getting fruits ready: Choose fresh, ripe, high quality fruits. Freezing only preserves quality; it does not improve it. Sort the fruit, removing those of inferior quality. Then wash in cold water; drain. Quickly peel, core, and cut up fruits. To avoid darkening during preparation, treat fruits with ascorbic acid color keeper or lemon juice and salt as directed in recipes in Canning and Freezing Guide (pages 84 to 89). Do not soak fruits.

Filling and sealing the containers: Consider how you will use the fruit to be frozen, then choose the best method of filling or packing the containers: syrup pack, sugar pack, or unsweetened pack (dry or water). Ascorbic acid color keeper is used in all packs to prevent undesirable chemical changes in susceptible fruits.

Pack fruits tightly in clean freezer containers following directions for syrup, sugar, or unsweetened pack in the Canning and Freezing Guide (pages 84 to 89). Leave proper headspace between the top of fruits and rim of the freezer container to allow room for expansion during freezing. The correct amount of headspace depends on the type of pack and freezer container used. For fruits packed in syrup, sugar, or water, leave ½ inch headspace when wide-mouth containers are used. When narrow-mouth containers are used with syrup, sugar, or water, leave ¾ inch for pints and 1½ inches for quarts. For dry-packed fruits, leave ½ inch headspace for all freezer containers. Seal dry-packed fruits in freezer bags by pressing out air and closing with a twist tie.

For syrup or unsweetened pack (water), add enough cold syrup or water to cover fruits, leaving the proper headspace. Syrups for canning and freezing are the same; prepare *very light, light, medium*, or *heavy syrup* ahead of time as directed on page 81 and chill. Syrup should be compatible with the sweetness of fruits.

To prevent surface discoloration place a crumpled piece of waxed paper or plastic wrap atop fruits to keep them covered in liquid. Seal containers; edges should be free from food, syrup, or moisture. Label containers with contents and date.

Storing the containers: Freeze containers in small batches at 0° or below. Leave room for air to circulate between containers. If properly frozen, fruits maintain quality for 8 to 12 months.

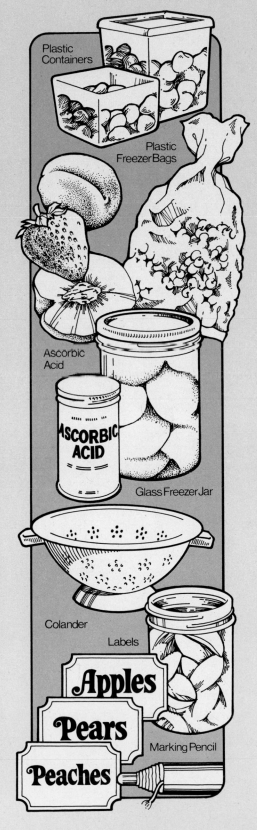

CANNING & FREEZING GUIDE

Apples

Preparation: Allow 2½ to 3 pounds *apples* for each quart. Rinse. Peel, core, and halve, quarter, or slice, removing stems and blossom ends.

Dip apples into *water* containing *ascorbic acid color keeper* or *salt* and *lemon juice*. (Follow package directions for proportions of color keeper to water or use 2 tablespoons salt and 2 tablespoons lemon juice for each gallon of water.) Drain well.

For freezing, if desired, steam apples for firmer texture. Place on rack above water in covered kettle. Bring to boiling. Steam for 2 minutes. Cool.

Canning: *hot pack:* In kettle prepare desired *syrup*. Allow 1 to 1½ cups syrup for each quart. Bring syrup to boiling; reduce heat. Prepare apples as above; add to syrup and return to boiling. Remove from heat. Spoon apples into hot, clean jars, leaving ½ inch headspace. Return syrup to boiling. Add enough boiling syrup to cover, leaving ½ inch headspace. Wipe rims; adjust lids. Process in boiling water bath for 20 minutes for pints or quarts (start timing when water boils).

Freezing: *unsweetened pack:* Prepare apples as above. Stir ½ teaspoon *ascorbic acid color keeper* into each 4 cups cold *water*. Allow 1 to 1½ cups water for each quart. Pack apples into moisture-vaporproof freezer containers, leaving proper headspace. Add enough water to cover apples, leaving proper headspace. Seal, label, and freeze.

Syrup pack: Prepare desired *syrup*; chill. Allow 1 to 1½ cups syrup for each quart. Prepare apples as above. Stir ½ teaspoon *ascorbic acid color keeper* into each 4 cups cold syrup. Pack apples into moisture-vaporproof freezer containers, leaving proper headspace. Add enough syrup to cover apples, leaving proper headspace. Seal, label, and freeze.

Sugar pack: Prepare apples as above. Dissolve ¼ teaspoon *ascorbic acid color keeper* in ¼ cup cold *water*. In large bowl sprinkle ascorbic acid color keeper mixture and ½ cup *sugar* over each 4 cups apples. Stir to mix. Pack apples tightly into moisture-vaporproof freezer containers, leaving proper headspace. Seal, label, and freeze.

Applesauce

8 pounds cooking apples, cored and quartered (24 cups)
1 to 1½ cups sugar

Preparation: In kettle combine apples and 2 cups *water*. If desired, add 10 inches stick cinnamon. Bring to boil. Cover and simmer for 8 to 10 minutes; stir often. Remove cinnamon. Press apples through food mill or sieve. Return pulp to kettle. Stir in sugar. If necessary, add ½ to 1 cup *water* for desired consistency. Bring to boil.

Canning: Prepare the applesauce as above. Spoon the boiling applesauce into hot, clean jars, leaving ½ inch headspace. Wipe rims; adjust lids. Process in boiling water bath for 20 minutes for pints or quarts (start timing when water boils). Makes 6 pints.

Freezing: Prepare applesauce as above. Cool. Spoon applesauce into moisture-vaporproof freezer containers, leaving proper headspace. Seal, label, and freeze. Makes 6 pints.

Apple Juice

10 pounds cooking apples, cored and coarsely chopped (36 cups)

Preparation: In kettle combine apples and 3 cups *water*. Bring to boil. Cover and simmer for 40 minutes; stir occasionally. Strain through jelly bag or several layers of cheesecloth. When cool, squeeze to extract remaining juice. Strain juice again; return to kettle. If desired, stir in 1 tablespoon sugar for each 2 cups juice. Bring to boil.

Canning: Prepare juice as above. Pour boiling juice into hot, clean jars, leaving ½ inch headspace. Wipe rims; adjust lids. Process in boiling water bath for 15 minutes for pints or quarts (start timing after water boils). Makes 3 to 4 pints.

Freezing: Prepare juice as above. Cool. Pour into moisture-vaporproof freezer containers, leaving proper headspace. Seal, label, and freeze. Makes 3 to 4 pints.

Apple Butter

6 pounds tart cooking apples, cored and
  quartered (18 cups)
5 cups apple cider *or* apple juice
1 cup cider vinegar
4 cups sugar
2 teaspoons ground cinnamon
½ teaspoon ground cloves
½ teaspoon ground allspice

Preparation: In kettle or Dutch oven combine apples, cider, and vinegar. Bring to boil. Cover; simmer for 30 minutes, stirring occasionally. Press through food mill or sieve. Measure 16 cups pulp. Return pulp to kettle or Dutch oven. Stir in remaining ingredients. Bring to boil. Simmer, uncovered, for 1½ to 2 hours or till very thick, stirring often.

Canning: Prepare butter as above. Spoon hot butter into hot, clean jars, leaving ½-inch headspace. Wipe jar rims; adjust lids. Process in boiling water bath for 10 minutes for half-pints or pints (start timing when water boils). Makes 8 to 9 half-pints.

Freezing: Prepare butter as above. Cool. Spoon butter into moisture-vaporproof freezer containers, leaving proper headspace. Seal, label, and freeze. Makes 8 to 9 half-pints.

Apricots

Preparation: Allow 1½ to 2½ pounds *apricots* (12 to 18 medium) for each quart. Thoroughly rinse apricots.

For freezing, peel apricots to prevent skins from toughening. Immerse whole apricots in *boiling water* for 20 to 30 seconds. Immediately plunge into cold *water* to stop cooking. (Do not allow apricots to soak in water.) Remove skins.

Halve and pit peeled or unpeeled apricots.

Prevent darkening during preparation by dipping the cut-up apricots into *water* containing *ascorbic acid color keeper* or *salt* and *lemon juice*. (Follow package directions for proportions of ascorbic acid color keeper to water, or use 2 tablespoons salt and 2 tablespoons lemon juice for each gallon of water.) Drain apricots well.

Canning: *cold pack:* Prepare desired *syrup*; allow 1 to 1½ cups syrup for each quart. Bring syrup to boiling; reduce heat. Prepare the apricots as above. Spoon the apricots into hot, clean jars, leaving ½ inch headspace. Return syrup to boiling. Add enough boiling syrup to cover apricots, leaving ½ inch headspace. Wipe jar rims; adjust lids. Process the apricots in boiling water for 25 minutes for pints or 30 minutes for quarts (start timing when water boils).

Hot pack: In kettle or Dutch oven prepare desired *syrup*; allow 1 to 1½ cups for each quart. Bring syrup to boiling; reduce heat. Prepare apricots as above; add to syrup and return to boiling. Remove from heat. Spoon apricots into hot, clean jars, leaving ½ inch headspace. Return syrup to boiling. Add boiling syrup to cover apricots, leaving ½ inch headspace. Wipe rims; adjust lids. Process in boiling water bath for 20 minutes for pints or 25 minutes for quarts (start timing when water boils).

Freezing: *syrup pack:* Prepare desired *syrup*; chill. Allow 1 to 1½ cups syrup for each quart. Prepare apricots as above. Stir ¾ teaspoon *ascorbic acid color keeper* into each 4 cups cold syrup. Pack apricots tightly into moisture-vaporproof freezer containers, leaving proper headspace. Add cold syrup to cover apricots, leaving proper headspace. Seal, label, and freeze.

Sugar pack: Prepare peeled apricots as above. Dissolve ¼ teaspoon *ascorbic acid color keeper* in ¼ cup cold *water*. In large bowl sprinkle ascorbic acid color keeper mixture and ½ cup *sugar* over each 4 cups apricots; stir. Pack tightly into moisture-vaporproof freezer containers, leaving proper headspace. Seal, label, and freeze.

Apricot-Honey Butter

2½ pounds apricots, halved and pitted
  (6 cups)
½ cup water
1½ cups sugar
½ cup honey
½ teaspoon finely shredded
  orange peel
2 tablespoons orange juice

Preparation: In 4- to 6-quart kettle combine apricots and water. Slowly bring to boiling. Cover and simmer for 5 to 10 minutes or till soft, stirring occasionally. Press apricot mixture through food mill or sieve. Measure 3 cups pulp. Return pulp to kettle. Stir in sugar, honey, orange peel, and orange juice. Bring to boiling. Reduce heat; boil gently, uncovered, for 30 to 35 minutes or till very thick, stirring occasionally.

Canning: Prepare butter as above. Spoon hot butter into hot, clean jars, leaving ½ inch headspace. Wipe jar rims; adjust lids. Process in boiling water bath for 10 minutes for half-pints or pints (start timing when water boils). Makes 3 to 4 half-pints.

Freezing: Prepare butter as above. Cool. Spoon into moisture-vaporproof freezer containers, leaving proper headspace. Seal, label, and freeze. Makes 3 to 4 half-pints.

Berries

Preparation: Allow 1½ to 3 pounds *blackberries, blueberries, boysenberries, gooseberries, huckleberries, loganberries, raspberries,* or *strawberries* for each quart. Strawberries are not recommended for canning because they fade, loose flavor, and do not retain their shape. Sort and rinse berries, removing stems and leaves; drain.

Canning: *cold pack:* (For use with soft berries such as blackberries, boysenberries, loganberries, and raspberries.) Prepare desired *syrup*, allowing 1 to 1½ cups for each quart. Bring to boiling; reduce heat. Prepare berries as above. Spoon into hot, clean jars, leaving ½ inch headspace. Lightly shake the jars to pack closely (do not crush). Return syrup to boiling. Add boiling syrup to cover the berries, leaving ½ inch headspace. Wipe jar rims; adjust lids. Process in boiling water bath for 15 minutes for pints or 20 minutes for quarts (start timing when water boils).

Hot pack: (For use with firm berries such as blueberries, gooseberries, and huckleberries.) Prepare berries as above. In kettle sprinkle ¼ to ½ cup *sugar* over each 4 cups berries. Gently stir berries to mix. Let stand for 30 minutes. Add ¼ cup *water* to each 4 cups berries. Slowly bring to boiling, stirring gently to dissolve sugar. Spoon into hot, clean jars, leaving ½ inch headspace. If there is not enough liquid to cover berries, add *boiling water* to cover, leaving ½ inch headspace. Wipe jar rims; adjust lids. Process in boiling water bath for 10 minutes for pints or 15 minutes for quarts (start timing when water boils).

Freezing: *unsweetened pack:* Prepare berries as directed above. If desired, slice strawberries. Pack berries into moisture-vaporproof freezer containers or bags, leaving proper headspace. Lightly shake to pack berries closely (do not crush). Seal, label, and freeze.

Syrup pack: Prepare desired *syrup*; chill. Allow 1 to 1½ cups syrup for each quart. Prepare berries as directed above. If desired, slice strawberries. Pack into moisture-vaporproof freezer containers, leaving proper headspace. Lightly shake the container to pack closely (do not crush). Add enough of the cold syrup to cover berries, leaving proper headspace. Seal, label, and freeze.

Sugar pack: Prepare berries as directed above. If desired, slice strawberries. In large bowl sprinkle ½ cup *sugar* over each 4 cups of berries. Gently stir berries to mix. If desired, let berries stand 30 minutes to dissolve sugar. Pack berries into moisture-vaporproof freezer containers, leaving proper headspace. Lightly shake the container to pack the berries closely (do not crush). Seal, label, and freeze.

Cherries

Preparation: Allow 2 to 2½ pounds unpitted *dark sweet* or *tart red cherries* for each quart. Sort and rinse cherries, removing stems and leaves. Drain well. If desired, pit cherries.

Canning: *cold pack:* Prepare desired *syrup*; allow 1 to 1½ cups of syrup for each quart. Bring syrup to boiling; reduce heat. Prepare cherries as above. Spoon cherries into hot, clean jars, leaving ½ inch headspace. Lightly shake jars to pack closely. Return syrup to boiling. Add enough boiling syrup to cover cherries, leaving ½ inch headspace. Wipe jar rims; adjust lids. Process cherries in boiling water bath for 20 minutes for pints or 25 minutes for quarts (start timing when water boils).

Hot pack: Prepare cherries as directed above. In kettle or Dutch oven sprinkle ⅔ to ¾ cup *sugar* over each 4 cups cherries. Gently stir to mix. Let stand for 2 hours. If additional juice is necessary, add about ¼ cup *water* to each 4 cups cherries. Slowly bring to boiling, stirring gently to dissolve sugar. Spoon cherry mixture into hot, clean jars, leaving ½ inch headspace. If there is not enough liquid to cover cherries, add *boiling water* to cover, leaving ½ inch headspace. Wipe jar rims; adjust lids. Process cherries in boiling water bath for 10 minutes for pints or 15 minutes for quarts (start timing when water boils).

Freezing: *unsweetened pack:* Prepare cherries as directed above. Dip cherries into *water* containing *ascorbic acid color keeper* (follow package directions for proportions of color keeper to water). Drain cherries well. Pack cherries into moisture-vaporproof freezer containers or bags, leaving proper headspace. Lightly shake containers or bags to pack cherries closely (do not crush). Seal, label, and freeze.

Syrup pack: Prepare desired *syrup*; chill. Allow 1 to 1½ cups syrup for each quart of cherries. Prepare cherries as directed above. Stir ½ teaspoon *ascorbic acid color keeper* into each 4 cups of cold syrup. Pack the cherries into moisture-vaporproof freezer containers, leaving the proper amount of headspace. Lightly shake containers to pack cherries closely (do not crush). Add enough cold syrup to cover cherries, leaving the proper amount of headspace. Seal, label, and freeze.

Sugar pack: Prepare cherries as directed above. Dissolve ¼ teaspoon *ascorbic acid color keeper* in ¼ cup cold *water*. In large bowl sprinkle color keeper mixture and ½ cup *sugar* over each 4 cups of cherries. Gently stir to mix. Pack cherries into moisture-vaporproof freezer containers, leaving the proper amount of headspace. Lightly shake container to pack cherries closely (do not crush). Seal, label, and freeze.

Brandied Sweet Cherries

2 pounds dark sweet cherries, pitted
2 cups sugar
  Brandy

Preparation: Combine cherries and sugar. Let stand 2 hours. Cover; cook over low heat 25 minutes; stir often. Remove cherries from syrup. Bring syrup to boil; boil, uncovered, 10 minutes. Measure syrup; add ⅓ cup brandy for each cup.
Canning: In kettle combine syrup and cherries. Bring to boiling. Spoon into hot, clean jars, leaving ½ inch headspace. Wipe rims; adjust lids. Process in boiling water bath for 20 minutes (start timing when water boils). Store at least 2 months before serving. Makes 4 to 5 half-pints.

Pickled Sweet Cherries

4 pounds dark sweet cherries, pitted
2 cups sugar
¾ cup vinegar
1 teaspoon ground cinnamon
½ teaspoon ground cloves

Preparation: In kettle combine all ingredients and 1 cup *water*. Bring to boil; simmer 5 minutes.
Canning: Return cherry mixture to boiling. Spoon into hot, clean jars, leaving ½ inch headspace. Wipe rims; adjust lids. Process in boiling water bath for 10 minutes (start timing when water boils). Makes 11 half-pints.

Grapes

Preparation: Allow 1½ to 2½ pounds *grapes* for each quart. Sort and rinse grapes, removing stems and leaves. If necessary, halve and seed grapes.
Canning: *cold pack:* Prepare desired *syrup*; allow 1 to 1½ cups for each quart. Bring syrup to boil. Prepare grapes as above. Spoon into hot, clean jars, leaving ½ inch headspace. Lightly shake. Add boiling syrup to cover, leaving ½ inch headspace. Wipe rims; adjust lids. Process in boiling water bath for 15 minutes for pints or 20 minutes for quarts (start timing when water boils).
Freezing: *syrup pack:* Prepare desired *syrup*; chill. Allow 1 to 1½ cups for each quart. Prepare grapes as above. Pack into moisture-vaporproof containers. Add syrup to cover; leave proper headspace. Seal, label, and freeze.

Grape Juice Concentrate

6 pounds Concord grapes (14 cups)
2 cups water
1½ cups sugar

Preparation: In 6-quart kettle or Dutch oven combine Concord grapes and water; cover. Bring to boiling. Reduce heat; cook over low heat about 30 minutes or till grapes are very tender, stirring occasionally. Remove grape mixture from heat; strain through a jelly bag or several layers of cheesecloth set in a colander. Discard grape seeds and skins. Chill the strained juice for 24 hours. Carefully strain the chilled juice again, leaving the sediment in bottom. In kettle or Dutch oven combine the strained grape juice and sugar; bring to boiling.
Canning: Prepare juice as above. Pour boiling juice into hot, clean jars, leaving ½ inch headspace. Wipe jar rims; adjust lids. Process the juice in boiling water bath for 10 minutes for pints (start timing when water boils). Makes 5 pints.
Freezing: Prepare juice as above. Cool. Pour the juice into moisture-vaporproof freezer containers, leaving proper headspace. Seal, label, and freeze. Makes 5 pints.
Serving: Dilute each pint of canned or frozen grape juice concentrate with 1 cup *water*. If necessary, add additional water to dilute concentrate to desired strength. Mix well. Cover and chill thoroughly before serving.

Melons

Preparation: Allow about 4 pounds of *cantaloupe, Crenshaw melon, honeydew melon, Persian melon,* or *watermelon* for each quart. If desired, use any combination of the melons. Halve, seed, and remove rind from melon. Cut melon into slices, cubes, or balls.
Freezing: *unsweetened pack:* Prepare melon as directed above. Pack the melon slices, cubes, or balls tightly into moisture-vaporproof freezer containers or freezer bags (do not crush), leaving proper headspace. Seal, label, and freeze. (Pictured on page 80).
  Syrup pack: Prepare desired *syrup*; chill thoroughly. Allow 1 to 1½ cups syrup for each quart of melon. Prepare melon as directed above. Pack the melon slices, cubes, or balls tightly into moisture-vaporproof freezer containers (do not crush), leaving proper headspace. Add enough cold syrup to cover melon, leaving proper headspace. Seal, label, and freeze.

Peaches

Preparation: Allow 1½ to 3 pounds *peaches* for each quart. Rinse peaches. To peel, immerse in *boiling water* for 20 to 30 seconds. Plunge into cold *water*. Remove skins. Halve and pit peaches.

Prevent darkening during preparation by dipping peaches into *water* containing *ascorbic acid color keeper* or *salt* and *lemon juice*. (Follow package directions for proportions of color keeper to water or use 2 tablespoons salt and 2 tablespoons lemon juice for each gallon of water.) Drain well.

Canning: *cold pack:* Prepare desired *syrup*; allow 1 to 1½ cups of syrup for each quart. Bring to boiling; reduce heat. Prepare peaches as above. Spoon peach halves, cavity side down and layers overlapping, into hot, clean jars, leaving ½ inch headspace. Return syrup to boiling. Add enough boiling syrup to cover peaches, leaving ½ inch headspace. Wipe jar rims; adjust lids. Process in boiling water bath for 25 minutes for pints or 30 minutes for quarts (start timing when water boils).

Hot pack: In kettle prepare desired *syrup*; allow 1 to 1½ cups for each quart. Bring to boiling; reduce heat. Prepare peaches as above; add to syrup and return to boiling. Remove from heat. Spoon peach halves, cavity side down and layers overlapping, into hot, clean jars, leaving ½ inch headspace. Return syrup to boiling. Add enough boiling syrup to cover peaches, leaving ½ inch headspace. Wipe rims; adjust lids. Process in boiling water bath for 20 minutes for pints or 25 minutes for quarts (start timing when water boils).

Freezing: *unsweetened pack:* Prepare peaches as above; slice, if desired. Stir 1 teaspoon *ascorbic acid color keeper* into each 4 cups cold *water*. Allow 1 to 1½ cups of the water for each quart. Pack peaches tightly into moisture-vaporproof freezer containers, leaving proper headspace. Add the water to cover, leaving proper headspace. Seal, label, and freeze.

Syrup pack: Prepare desired *syrup*; chill. Allow 1 to 1½ cups syrup for each quart. Prepare peaches as above; slice, if desired. Stir ½ teaspoon *ascorbic acid color keeper* into each 4 cups of cold syrup. Pack peaches tightly into moisture-vaporproof freezer containers, leaving proper headspace. Add enough cold syrup to cover, leaving proper headspace. Seal, label, and freeze.

Sugar pack: Prepare peaches as above; slice, if desired. Dissolve ¼ teaspoon *ascorbic acid color keeper* in ¼ cup cold *water*. Sprinkle ascorbic acid color keeper mixture and ½ cup *sugar* over each 4 cups of peaches. Stir to mix. Pack peaches tightly into moisture-vaporproof freezer containers, leaving proper headspace. Seal, label, and freeze.

Spiced Peaches
(pictured on page 80)

5 **cups sugar**
1 **cup vinegar**
12 **inches stick cinnamon, broken**
2 **teaspoons whole cloves**
5 **pounds small peaches**

Preparation: For syrup, in kettle combine sugar, vinegar, cinnamon, cloves, and 2 cups *water*. Bring to boiling; reduce heat. Peel peaches. If desired, halve and pit. To prevent darkening, add peaches to syrup as soon as they are peeled. Simmer about 5 minutes. Remove from heat.

Canning: Spoon peaches into hot, clean jars, leaving ½ inch headspace. Return syrup to boiling. Add boiling syrup to cover, leaving ½ inch headspace. Wipe rims; adjust lids. Process in boiling water bath for 20 minutes (start timing when water boils). Makes 5 or 6 pints.

Pears

Preparation: Allow 2 to 3 pounds *pears* for each quart. Rinse pears; peel, halve, and core, removing stems and blossom ends. Do not freeze pears.

Prevent darkening during preparation by dipping pears into *water* containing *ascorbic acid color keeper* or *salt* and *lemon juice*. (Follow package directions for proportions of color keeper to water or use 2 tablespoons salt and 2 tablespoons lemon juice for each gallon of water.) Drain.

Canning: *cold pack:* Prepare desired *syrup*; allow 1 to 1½ cups syrup for each quart. Bring to boiling; reduce heat. Prepare pears as above. Spoon pear halves, cavity side down and layers overlapping, into hot, clean jars; leave ½ inch headspace. Return syrup to boiling. Add boiling syrup to cover pears, leaving ½ inch headspace. Wipe rims; adjust lids. Process in boiling water bath for 25 minutes for pints or 30 minutes for quarts (start timing when water boils).

Hot pack: In kettle prepare desired *syrup*; allow 1 to 1½ cups for each quart. Bring to boiling; reduce heat. Prepare pears as above; add to syrup and return to boiling. Remove from heat. Spoon pear halves, cavity side down and layers overlapping, into hot, clean jars, leaving ½ inch headspace. Return syrup to boiling. Add boiling syrup to cover pears, leaving ½ inch headspace. Wipe rims; adjust lids. Process in boiling water bath for 20 minutes for pints or 25 minutes for quarts (start timing when water boils).

Minted Pears

4 cups water
1 cup sugar
⅔ cup green crème de menthe liqueur
  Few drops green food coloring (optional)
7 pounds pears

Preparation: For syrup, in kettle or Dutch oven combine water and sugar. Bring to boiling; reduce heat. Stir in crème de menthe. If desired, stir in green food coloring. Peel, halve, and core pears. To prevent darkening, add pears to syrup as they are cut. Bring to boiling. Remove from heat.

Canning: Spoon pear halves, cavity side down and layers overlapping, into hot, clean jars, leaving ½ inch headspace. Return syrup to boiling. Add enough boiling syrup to cover pears, leaving ½ inch headspace. Wipe jar rims; adjust lids. Process in boiling water bath for 20 minutes for pints or 25 minutes for quarts (start timing when water boils). Makes 7 pints.

Plums

Preparation: Allow 1¼ to 2½ pounds of *plums* for each quart. Thoroughly rinse plums and remove stems. Drain well. Prick plum skins. For freezing, halve and pit plums.

Canning: *cold pack:* Prepare desired *syrup*; allow about 1 to 1½ cups for each quart. Bring syrup to boiling; reduce heat. Prepare plums as above. Spoon plums into hot, clean jars, leaving ½ inch headspace. Return syrup to boiling. Add enough boiling syrup to cover plums, leaving ½ inch headspace. Wipe jar rims; adjust lids. Process in boiling water bath for 20 minutes for pints or 25 minutes for quarts (start timing when water boils).

Hot pack: In kettle prepare desired *syrup*. Allow 1 to 1½ cups syrup for each quart. Bring syrup to boiling; reduce heat. Prepare plums as above; add to syrup and return to boiling. Simmer for 2 minutes. Remove from heat. Cover and let stand for 20 to 30 minutes. Spoon plums into hot, clean jars, leaving ½ inch headspace. Return syrup to boiling. Add enough boiling syrup to cover plums, leaving ½ inch headspace. Wipe jar rims; adjust lids. Process in boiling water bath for 20 minutes for pints or 25 minutes for quarts (start timing when water boils).

Freezing: *unsweetened pack:* Prepare plums as above. Dip halved plums into *water* containing *ascorbic acid color keeper*. (Follow package directions for proportions of color keeper to water.) Drain well. Pack plums tightly into moisture-vaporproof freezer containers or bags, leaving proper headspace. Seal, label, and freeze.

Syrup pack: Prepare desired *syrup*; chill. Allow 1 to 1½ cups syrup for each quart. Prepare plums as above. Stir ½ teaspoon *ascorbic acid color keeper* into each 4 cups cold syrup. Pack plums into moisture-vaporproof freezer containers, leaving proper headspace. Add cold syrup to cover plums, leaving proper amount of headspace. Seal, label, and freeze.

Sugar pack: Prepare plums as above. Dissolve ¼ teaspoon *ascorbic acid color keeper* in ¼ cup cold *water*. In large bowl sprinkle ascorbic acid color keeper mixture and ½ cup *sugar* over each 4 cups of plums. Stir to mix. Pack plums tightly into moisture-vaporproof freezer containers, leaving proper headspace. Seal, label, and freeze.

Rhubarb

Preparation: Allow 1 to 2 pounds *rhubarb* for each quart. Discard woody ends and leaves. Rinse rhubarb; drain. Slice stalks into ½-inch pieces.

For freezing, blanch rhubarb. To blanch, immerse rhubarb pieces into boiling water. Cover; boil for 1 minute. Immediately plunge into cold water for 1 minute. Drain well.

Canning: *hot pack:* Prepare rhubarb as above. In kettle sprinkle ½ to 1 cup *sugar* over each 4 cups rhubarb pieces. Mix well. Let stand about 1 hour. Slowly bring to boil; simmer for 1 minute. Remove from heat. Spoon into hot, clean jars, leaving ½ inch headspace. Wipe rims; adjust lids. Process in boiling water bath for 10 minutes for half-pints or pints (start timing when water boils).

Freezing: *unsweetened pack:* Prepare rhubarb as above. Pack blanched rhubarb pieces into moisture-vaporproof freezer containers or bags, leaving proper headspace. Lightly shake to pack rhubarb closely. Seal, label, and freeze.

Syrup pack: Prepare desired *syrup*; chill thoroughly. Allow 1 to 1½ cups syrup for each quart. Prepare rhubarb as above. Pack blanched rhubarb pieces into moisture-vaporproof freezer containers, leaving proper headspace. Lightly shake to pack rhubarb closely. Add enough cold syrup to cover rhubarb, leaving proper headspace. Seal, label, and freeze.

Sugar pack: Prepare rhubarb as above. Sprinkle ½ cup *sugar* over each 3 cups blanched rhubarb pieces (4 cups raw). Stir to mix and dissolve sugar. Pack tightly into moisture-vaporproof freezer containers, leaving proper headspace. Lightly shake to pack rhubarb closely. Seal, label, and freeze.

JELLY & JAM BASICS

To prepare juice for jelly, strain cooked fruit mixture through jelly bag or several layers of cheesecloth.

To test for jellying stage, dip a metal spoon in jelly. Watch for 2 drops that sheet together off spoon.

Using a wide-mouth funnel, ladle or pour boiling jelly into jars, filling to within ¼ inch of the top.

There's nothing quite like a spoonful of homemade jelly spread on a toasted muffin to brighten the morning. But don't stop with homemade jelly. We have basic directions and a smattering of recipes for jams, preserves, conserves, and marmalades, too.

Assembling the equipment: Useful equipment includes an 8- to 10-quart kettle or Dutch oven, an accurate thermometer, and a jelly bag or cheesecloth and colander for straining juice for jelly.

Jars should be free from cracks or nicks. Paraffin or flat metal lids and screw bands may be used for sealing jars of jelly. In contrast, jams and other spreads must be sealed in standard half-pint canning jars with flat metal lids and screw bands for the requisite water bath processing. That makes a boiling water bath canner, complete with rack, essential for jam-type spreads.

Preparing jelly: Wash jars in sudsy water; rinse. Sterilize in boiling water for 10 minutes. Let stand in water till ready to fill; drain. Prepare lids according to manufacturer's directions; or, if using paraffin, melt over hot water. Techniques for preparing jelly vary. For jelly without added pectin, juice is prepared, then cooked with sugar till jellying point is reached (see illustrations at left and recipe directions). A thermometer is useful for measuring the jellying point which is 8° above the boiling point of water (220° at sea level). For jelly with added pectin, it is not necessary to cook to jellying point (see recipe directions). After cooking with or without added pectin, remove from heat; quickly skim off foam with metal spoon. Using a wide-mouth funnel, ladle or pour jelly into hot, sterilized jars, leaving ¼ inch headspace. Wipe jar rims.

Sealing jelly: To seal with flat metal lids and screw bands, place lid with sealing compound next to glass; screw band down firmly. Invert jar for a few seconds to sterilize lid. Turn right side up; cool. When cool, check seal by feeling for indentation in center of lid. Label; store in cool, dry place. To seal with paraffin, spoon thin layer of melted paraffin over surface of hot jelly. Rotate jar so paraffin clings to sides. Prick any air bubbles. After paraffin hardens, spoon another thin layer over to total depth of ⅛ inch. Cool. Label; cover paraffin. Store in cool, dry place.

Preparing jam, preserves, conserves, and marmalade: Wash jars and lids in sudsy water; rinse in hot water. Let stand in water till ready to fill, then drain. Place rack in water bath canner; fill with 4 to 5 inches of water. Cover and heat. At same time heat additional water. Procedures differ slightly for cooking various jam-type spreads (see recipe directions). Using a wide-mouth funnel, ladle or pour cooked product into hot, clean jars, leaving ¼ inch headspace. Wipe rims. Place lid with sealing compound next to glass; screw metal band down firmly.

Processing jam, preserves, conserves, and marmalade: Place sealed jars on rack in water bath canner; add boiling water till level is 1 to 2 inches above tops of jars. Cover; continue heating till water boils. Once the water is boiling, start counting the 15 minutes of processing time. While the jars are cooling, invert them for 30 minutes to prevent fruit from floating. When jars are completely cool, check seals by feeling for an indentation in center of lid. Label and store in cool, dry place.

JELLY & JAM RECIPES

Apple Jelly

3 pounds tart apples, cut into chunks
3 cups sugar

In 8- to 10-quart kettle combine apples and 5 cups *water*. Bring to boiling. Cover; simmer about 30 minutes or till very soft, stirring occasionally.

Strain through jelly bag or several layers of cheesecloth; do not squeeze. Measure juice. Add enough water to measure 4 cups liquid. In kettle heat and stir apple juice and sugar till dissolved. Bring to full rolling boil (a boil that cannot be stirred down). Boil hard, uncovered, for 11 to 13 minutes or till syrup sheets off metal spoon. Remove from heat; quickly skim off foam with metal spoon. Ladle syrup into hot, sterilized jars, leaving ¼ inch headspace. Seal jars using metal lids or paraffin. Makes 4 half-pints.

Cinnamon-Apple Jelly: Prepare as directed above, *except* add 4 to 6 inches stick *cinnamon*, broken, to kettle with apple juice and sugar. Remove cinnamon before skimming off foam.

Mint-Apple Jelly: Prepare as directed above, *except* tie 1 cup lightly packed fresh *mint leaves* in cheesecloth bag; press mint with rolling pin to bruise leaves. Add bruised leaves and 6 drops *green food coloring* to kettle with juice and sugar. Remove leaves before skimming off foam.

Fruit Juice Jelly

(pictured on page 80)

4 cups unsweetened apple, grape, orange, *or* pineapple juice *or* cranberry juice cocktail (not low-calorie)
1 1¾-ounce package powdered fruit pectin
¼ cup lemon juice
4½ cups sugar

In 8- to 10-quart kettle combine fruit juice, pectin, and lemon juice. Bring to full rolling boil (a boil that cannot be stirred down). Stir in sugar. Return to full rolling boil. Boil hard, uncovered, for 1 minute; stir constantly. Remove from heat; quickly skim off foam with metal spoon. Ladle fruit syrup at once into hot, sterilized jars, leaving ¼ inch headspace. Seal jars using metal lids or paraffin. Makes 6 half-pints.

Grape Jelly

3½ pounds Concord grapes, stemmed (10 cups)
½ cup water
3 cups sugar

Crush grapes; measure 6½ cups. In 8- to 10-quart kettle or Dutch oven combine 6½ cups crushed grapes and water. Bring to boiling. Reduce heat; cover and simmer for 10 to 15 minutes or till grapes are very soft, stirring occasionally.

Strain grape mixture through jelly bag or several layers of cheesecloth set in colander; do not squeeze. If necessary, press very gently. Chill strained juice overnight.

Strain chilled juice to remove crystals. Measure juice. If necessary, add enough water to measure 4 cups liquid. In kettle or Dutch oven heat and stir grape juice and sugar till dissolved. Bring to full rolling boil (a boil that cannot be stirred down). Boil hard, uncovered, for 8 to 9 minutes or till syrup sheets off metal spoon. Remove from heat; quickly skim off foam with metal spoon. Ladle at once into hot, sterilized jars, leaving ¼ inch headspace. Seal using metal lids or paraffin. Makes 4 half-pints.

Freezer Jam

4 cups blackberries, raspberries, *or* strawberries, caps removed
4 cups sugar
¼ teaspoon ground nutmeg
½ of 6-ounce package (1 foil pouch) liquid fruit pectin
2 tablespoons lemon juice

Crush blackberries, raspberries, or strawberries; measure 2 cups. In large bowl combine 2 cups crushed berries, the sugar, and nutmeg. Let stand for 10 minutes.

Combine pectin and lemon juice. Add to the berry mixture; stir for 3 minutes. Ladle at once into clean half-pint jars or glasses or moisture-vapor-proof freezer containers, leaving ½ inch headspace. Seal and label. Let stand for several hours at room temperature or till jam is set. Store jam up to 3 weeks in refrigerator or 1 year in the freezer. Makes 5 half-pints.

Strawberry Jam

  8 **cups strawberries, caps removed**
  1 **1¾-ounce package powdered fruit pectin**
  2 **tablespoons lemon juice**
  7 **cups sugar**

In large bowl crush strawberries; measure 4½ cups of crushed strawberries.

   In 8- to 10-quart kettle or Dutch oven combine 4½ cups crushed strawberries, pectin, and lemon juice. Bring to full rolling boil (a boil that cannot be stirred down). Stir in sugar. Return to full rolling boil. Boil hard, uncovered, for 1 minute, stirring constantly. Remove from heat; quickly skim off foam with metal spoon. Ladle at once into hot, clean half-pint jars, leaving ¼ inch headspace. Wipe jar rims; adjust lids. Process in boiling water bath for 15 minutes (start timing when water returns to boiling). Makes 7 to 8 half-pints

Spiced Strawberry Jam: Prepare as directed above, *except* stir 1½ teaspoons ground *cinnamon* and 1 teaspoon ground *nutmeg* into strawberry mixture along with sugar.

Cherry-Raspberry Jam
(pictured on page 80)

1½ **pounds dark sweet *or* tart red cherries,
     stems removed**
  4 **cups red raspberries**
  7 **cups sugar**
  2 **tablespoons lemon juice**
 ½ **of a 6-ounce package (1 foil pouch) liquid
     fruit pectin**

Pit and coarsely chop dark sweet or tart red cherries; measure 2 cups coarsely chopped cherries. Crush red raspberries; measure 3 cups crushed raspberries.

   In 8- to 10-quart kettle combine 2 cups chopped cherries, 3 cups crushed raspberries, sugar, and lemon juice. Bring mixture to a full rolling boil (a boil that cannot be stirred down). Boil hard, uncovered, for 1 minute, stirring constantly. Remove from heat. Stir in liquid fruit pectin. Quickly skim off foam with metal spoon. Ladle at once into hot, clean half-pint jars, leaving ¼ inch headspace. Wipe jar rims; adjust lids. Process in boiling water bath for 15 minutes (start timing when water returns to boiling). Makes 8 to 9 half-pints.

Peach Jam

2½ **to 3 pounds peaches (10 to 12 medium)**
  1 **1¾-ounce package powdered fruit pectin**
  2 **tablespoons lemon juice**
5½ **cups sugar**

Peel, pit, and coarsely grind peaches; measure 4 cups ground peaches.

   In 8- to 10-quart kettle or Dutch oven combine 4 cups ground peaches, pectin, and lemon juice. Bring to full rolling boil (a boil that cannot be stirred down), stirring constantly. Stir in sugar. Return to full rolling boil. Boil hard, uncovered, for 1 minute, stirring constantly. Remove from heat; quickly skim off foam with metal spoon. Ladle at once into hot, clean half-pint jars, leaving ¼ inch headspace. Wipe jar rims; adjust lids. Process in boiling water bath for 15 minutes (start timing when water returns to boiling). Makes 6 to 7 half-pints.

Peach-Banana Jam: Prepare jam as directed above *except* chop 1 slightly green medium *banana* and add to kettle or Dutch oven with peaches, pectin, and lemon juice.

Peach-Plum Jam: Prepare jam as directed above *except* coarsely grind 1¼ *pounds* of peaches (5 to 6 medium); measure *2 cups* ground peaches. Pit and finely chop ¾ pound fully ripe *Italian prune plums* (about 12 medium); measure 2 cups. Add plums to kettle or Dutch oven with peaches, pectin, and lemon juice.

Plum Jam

3 **pounds red plums (about 22 medium)**
3 **cups sugar**
2 **tablespoons lemon juice**

Halve, pit, and coarsely grind plums; measure 4 cups ground plums.

   In 8- to 10-quart kettle or Dutch oven combine 4 cups ground plums, sugar, and lemon juice. Let mixture stand for 1 hour. Bring mixture to a full rolling boil (a boil that cannot be stirred down). Boil hard, uncovered, for 16 minutes or till syrup sheets off metal spoon. Remove from heat; quickly skim off foam with metal spoon. Ladle at once into hot, clean, half-pint jars, leaving ¼ inch headspace. Wipe jar rims; adjust lids. Process in boiling water bath for 15 minutes (start timing when water boils). Makes 4 to 5 half-pints.

Apricot-Pear Jam

3 pounds apricots (about 30 medium)
2 pounds Bartlett pears (about 8 medium)
6 cups sugar
1 tablespoon finely shredded orange peel
⅓ cup orange juice
¼ teaspoon ground nutmeg or ¼ teaspoon ground mace

Peel and pit apricots. Finely chop apricots; measure 4½ cups. Core and quarter pears. Finely chop pears; measure 4 cups.

In 8- to 10-quart kettle or Dutch oven combine apricots, pears, sugar, orange peel, and orange juice. Slowly bring mixture to full rolling boil (a boil that cannot be stirred down), stirring constantly. Boil hard, uncovered, for 20 to 25 minutes or till syrup sheets off metal spoon. Remove from heat. Stir in nutmeg or mace. Quickly skim off foam with metal spoon. Ladle at once into hot, clean, half-pint jars, leaving ¼ inch headspace. Wipe jar rims; adjust lids. Process in boiling water bath for 15 minutes (start timing when water returns to boiling). Makes 8 to 9 half-pints.

Mixed Fruit Conserve

1½ pounds peaches (about 6 medium)
1 pound pears (about 4 medium)
¾ pound red plums (about 5 medium)
4 cups sugar
1 cup raisins
½ cup chopped nuts
¼ cup lemon juice

Peel, pit, and dice peaches; measure 3 cups. Peel, core, and dice pears; measure 2 cups. Pit and dice plums; measure 2 cups.

In 8- to 10-quart kettle or Dutch oven combine peaches, pears, plums, sugar, and raisins. Heat and stir till sugar dissolves. Bring fruit mixture to full rolling boil. Boil hard, uncovered, for 15 to 18 minutes or till syrup sheets from metal spoon, stirring constantly. Stir in nuts and lemon juice. Remove from heat. Skim off foam with metal spoon. Ladle at once into hot, clean, half-pint jars, leaving ¼ inch headspace. Wipe jar rims; adjust lids. Process in boiling water bath for 15 minutes (start timing when water returns to boiling). Makes 6 to 7 half-pints.

Orange Marmalade

4 medium oranges
1 medium lemon
⅛ teaspoon baking soda
5 cups sugar
½ of a 6-ounce package (1 foil pouch) liquid fruit pectin

Score orange and lemon peels into 4 lengthwise sections. Remove peels; scrape off white portion. Cut peels into very thin strips. Combine peels, soda, and 1½ cups water. Bring to boiling. Cover; simmer for 10 minutes. Do not drain. Remove membrane from fruits. Section fruits, reserving juices; discard seeds. Add sectioned fruits and juices to peel. Return to boiling. Cover and simmer for 20 minutes. Measure 3 cups.

In 8- to 10-quart kettle combine 3 cups fruit mixture and sugar. Bring to full rolling boil; boil, uncovered, for 1 minute. Remove from heat; stir in pectin. Skim off foam. Ladle into hot, clean half-pint jars; leaving ¼ inch headspace. Wipe rims; adjust lids. Process in boiling water bath 15 minutes (start timing when water returns to boiling). Makes 5 to 6 half-pints.

Apple-Grapefruit Marmalade
(pictured on page 80)

2 medium grapefruits
⅛ teaspoon baking soda
2¾ pounds apples (about 8 medium)
3 tablespoons lemon juice
7 cups sugar
½ of a 6-ounce package (1 foil pouch) liquid fruit pectin

Score grapefruit peel into 6 lengthwise sections. Remove peel; scrape off white portion. Cut peel into very thin strips. Combine peel, soda, and 1½ cups water. Bring to boil. Cover and simmer for 20 minutes; stir occasionally; drain. Remove membrane from grapefruits. Section grapefruits; discard seeds. Chop sections.

Peel, core, and coarsely chop apples. In 8- to 10-quart kettle combine cooked peel, grapefruits, apples, lemon juice, and 1 cup water. Bring to boiling. Simmer, uncovered, 10 minutes. Stir in sugar. Bring to full rolling boil; stir constantly. Boil 1 minute. Remove from heat; stir in pectin. Skim off foam. Stir and skim for 10 minutes. Pour into hot, clean half-pint jars, leaving ¼ inch headspace. Wipe jar rims; adjust lids. Process in boiling water bath for 15 minutes (start timing when water returns to boiling). Makes 8 to 9 half-pints.

INDEX